Transfer of Title Concerning Movables Part II –
Eigentumsübertragung an beweglichen Sachen in Europa Teil II

Mary-Rose McGuire

Transfer of Title Concerning Movables Part II – Eigentumsübertragung an beweglichen Sachen in Europa Teil II

National Report: Germany

Edited by Johannes Michael Rainer –
Herausgegeben von Johannes Michael Rainer

PETER LANG
Europäischer Verlag der Wissenschaften

Salzburger Studien zum Europäischen Privatrecht

Herausgegeben von Prof. DDr. J. Michael Rainer

Band 19

PETER LANG
Frankfurt am Main · Berlin · Bern · Bruxelles · New York · Oxford · Wien

Bibliographic Information published by Die Deutsche Bibliothek
Die Deutsche Bibliothek lists this publication in the Deutsche Nationalbibliografie; detailed bibliographic data is available in the internet at <http://dnb.ddb.de>.

The appearance of this book was made possible by the Austrian Science Fund FWF.

ISSN 1435-6090
ISBN 3-631-53950-9
US-ISBN 0-8204-7728-X

www.peterlang.de

Dr. Mary-Rose McGuire, M.Jur (Göttingen)
European Legal Studies Institute
Heger-Tor-Wall 12
D-49074 Osnabrück
mmcguire@uos.de

Acknowledgment

The following text on transfer of title under German law is both an overview and a response to the questionnaire of the Salzburg Working Team of the Study Group on European Civil Code on the project 'Transfer of Title'. Both content and order of the subjects dealt with therefore find their reason in the questionnaire and may differ from traditional textbooks on German law on movable property.

Only a minor part of the enormous amount of literature on the subject could be taken into account on providing this response, but I hope that the sources cited are representative for the German legal doctrine. The same caveat has to be made for the judicature cited: it is only a very rough outline and many more interesting cases have remained unmentioned.

As far as the text of the German Civil Code is reproduced, the translations rely on the translation provided on the website of the German Federal Ministry of Justice. As they do not give any further reference by whom the different paragraphs were translated, but instead merely mention that they have drawn from several different sources, I have not marked the translation with a footnote. However, I would like to acknowledge that the main source of the translation provided on the website seems to be an updated version of 'The German Civil Code' revised edition 1994 by *Simon L. Goren*. All provisions literally reproduced in the following text therefore are not my own translations but – although with adaptations – are taken from the homepage www.bmj.de.

I would like to express my gratitude to Professor Rainer for the possibility to publish this report in his series '*Salzburger Studien zum Europäischen Privatecht*'. Also I would like to thank *Thomas McGuire* and *Friederike Schäfer*, who were so kind to proofread the text and assist with the choice of literature.

Osnabrück, February 2005

Table of Contents

List of Abbreviations

ABGB	Allgemeines Bürgerliches Gesetzbuch (Civil Code, Austria)
AcP	Archiv für Civilistische Praxis
ALR	Preußisches Allgemeines Landrecht
AP	Nachschlagewerk des Bundesarbeitsgerichts
AT	Allgemeiner Teil
BayObLG	Bayrisches Oberstes Landgericht
BB	Betriebsberater
BGB	Bürgerliches Gesetzbuch (Civil Code, Germany)
BGBl	Bundesgesetzblatt (Official Journal of the Federal Republic of Germany)
BGH	Bundesgerichtshof (Federal Supreme Court)
BGHZ	Entscheidungen des Bundesgerichtshofs in Zivilrechtssachen (Case Reports of the Federal Supreme Court in Civil Matters)
BVerfG	Bundesverfassungsgericht (Federal Constitutional Court)
BVerfGE	Entscheidungen des Bundesverfassungsgerichts (Case Reports of the Federal Constitutional Court)
FamRZ	Zeitschrift für das gesamte Familienrecht
FS	Festschrift (*liber amoricum*)
GG	Grundgesetz (Basic Law, German Constitutional Act)
HGB	Handelsgesetzbuch
InsO	Insolvenzordnung (Insolvency Act)
JR	Juristische Rundschau
JuS	Juristische Schulung
JZ	Juristenzeitung
KTS	Zeitschrift für Konkurs, Treuhand und Insolvenz
LG	Landgericht (Regional Court)
LM	Lindenmaier/Möhring, Nachschlagewerk des Bundesgerichtshofs
MDR	Monatsschrift für deutsches Recht
NJW	Neue Juristische Wochenschrift

NVwZ	Neue Zeitschrift für Verwaltungsrecht
OLG	Oberlandesgericht (Higher Regional Court)
RabelsZ	Rabels Zeitschrift für Rechtsvergleichung
RG	Reichsgericht (pre-1945 German Supreme Court)
RGZ	Entscheidungen des Reichsgerichts in Zivilrechtssachen (Case Reports of the Reichsgericht in Civil Matters)
ZEuP	Zeitschrift für Europäisches Privatrecht
ZfRV	Zeitschrift für Rechtsvergleichung
ZIP	Zeitschrift für Wirtschaftsrecht und Insolvenzpraxis
ZPO	Zivilprozessordnung (Civil Procedure Code)

List of Authorities

Armbrüster, Christian	Eigentumsschtutz durch den Beseitigungsanspruch nach § 1004 I 1 BGB und durch Deliktsrecht, NJW 2003, 3087-3090.
Avenarius, Martin	Übereignung besitzloser Sachen und Vindikationszession, JZ 1994, 511-512.
Baldus, Christian	Abhandenkommen und ‚genereller Besitzwillen', JR 2002, 441-444.
Baur, Jürgen / Stürner, Rolf	Sachenrecht, 17th edition, Munich 1999.
Bork, Reinhard	Einführung in das Insolvenzrecht, 3rd edition, Tübingen 2002.
Braun, Johann	§ 935 I 2 BGB ist zu eng formuliert, JZ 1993, 391-396.
Brehm, Wolfgang / Berger, Christian	Sachenrecht, Tübingen 2000.
Canaris, Claus-Wilhelm	Die Verdinglichung obligatorischer Rechte, in liber amoricum Werner Flume, edited by Horst H. Jakobs et al., Cologne 1978, 371-427.
Depenheuer, Otto	Der Mieter als Eigentümer?, NJW 1993, 2561-2564.
Derleder, Peter	Auslegung und Umdeutung defizitärer mobiliarsachenrechtlicher Übereignungsabreden, JZ 1999, 176-183.
Eisenhardt, Ulrich	Die Einheitlichkeit des Rechtsgeschäfts und die Überwindung des Abstraktionsprinzips, JZ 1991, 271-277.
Ernst, Wolfgang	Anmerkung zu BGH 24.6.1987, JZ 1988, 359-361.
Feuerborn, Andreas	Der Bestimmtheitsgrundsatz bei der Übereignung von Sachgesamtheiten, ZIP 2001, 600-603.
Finkenauer, Thomas	Gutgläubiger Erwerb des bösgläubigen Erben – Das Bernsteinzimmermosaik, NJW 1998, 960-962.
Flume, Werner	Zur Problematik des verlängerten Eigentumsvorbehalts, NJW 1959, 913-922.
Flume, Werner	Der verlängerte und erweiterte Eigentumsvorbehalt, NJW 1950, 841-850.

Georgiades, Apostolos Eigentumsbegriff und Eigentumsverhältnis, in: Beiträge zur europäischen Rechtsgeschichte und zum geltenden Zivilrecht, Festschrift für Johannes Sontis, edited by Fritz Baur et al., Munich 1977, 149-166.

Gerhardt, Walter Mobiliarsachenrecht, 5th edition, Munich 2000.

Goren, Simon L. The German Civil Code, Rivised Edition, Translation with an Introduction, Littleton 1994.

Grunsky, Wolfgang Sicherungsübereignung, Sicherungsabtretung und Eigentumsvorbehalt in der Zwangsvollstreckung und im Konkurs des Schuldners, JuS 1984, 497-504.

Gursky, Karl-Heinz Die neue höchstrichterliche Rechtsprechung zum Mobiliarsachenrecht – Teil 1, JZ 1991, 496-503.

Gursky, Karl-Heinz Die neue höchstrichterliche Rechtsprechung zum Mobiliarsachenrecht – Teil 2, JZ 1991, 650-657.

Gursky, Karl-Heinz Die neue höchstrichterliche Rechtsprechung zum Mobiliarsachenrecht – Teil 1, JZ 1997, 1094-1104.

Gursky, Karl-Heinz Die neue höchstrichterliche Rechtsprechung zum Mobiliarsachenrecht – Teil 2, JZ 1997, 1154-1166.

Habersack, Matthias / Schürnbrand, Jan Der Eigentumsvorbehalt nach der Schuldrechtsreform JuS 2002, 833-839.

Hadding, Walther Rechtsverhältnis zwischen Person und Sache?, JZ 1986, 926-928.

Hadding, Walther Die Eigentumsvermutung nach § 1006 I BGB im Herausgaberechtsstreit – BGH FamRZ 1970, 586, JuS 1972, 183-185.

Hager, Johannes Streckengeschäft und redlicher Erwerb, ZIP 1993, 1446-1452.

Heck, Philipp Grundriß des Sachenrechts, 2nd edition, Tübingen 1930.

Heuer, Carl-Heinz Die Kunstraubzüge der Nationalsozialisten und ihre Rückabwicklung, NJW 1999, 2558-2564.

Huber, Michael Rücktrittsrecht des Vorbehaltsverkäufers in der Insolvenz des Vorbehaltskäufers, NZI 2004, 57-63.

Jahr, Günther Romanistische Beiträge zur modernen Zivilrechtswissenschaft, AcP 168 (1968), 9-27.

Jauernig, Othmar Trennungsprinzip und Abstraktionsprinzip, JuS 1994, 721-727.

Karner, Ernst Der redliche Mobiliarerwerb aus rechtsvergleichender und rechtsgeschichtlicher Perspektive, ZfRV 2004, 83-93.

Kindl, Johann Gutgläubiger Mobiliarerwerb und Erlangung mittelbaren Besitzes, AcP 201 (2001), 391-410.

Kirchhof, Hans-Peter / Lwowski, Hans-Jürgen / Stürner, Rolf (eds.) Münchener Kommentar zur Insolvenzordnung, Band I, § 1 - § 102, Munich 2001.

Krämer, Gerd Bernsteinzimmer-Mosaik – Ersitzung durch den gutgläubigen Erben des bösgläubigen Besitzers, NJW 1997, 2580-2581.

Larenz, Karl Canaris, Claus-Wilhelm Lehrbuch des Schuldrechts, Besonderer Teil, Band II/1, 13th edition, Munich 1986.

Larenz, Karl / Wolf, Manfred Allgemeiner Teil des Bürgerlichen Rechts, 9th edition, Munich 2004.

Lehmann-Richter, Arnold Possessorische Besitzschutzansprüche und petitorische Einwendungen im einstweiligen Rechtsschutz, NJW 2003, 1717-1718.

Mager, Heinrich Besonderheiten des dinglichen Anspruchs, AcP 193 (1993), 68-85.

Martinek, Michael Traditionsprinzip und Geheißerwerb, AcP 188 (1988), 573-648.

Marotzke, Wolfgang Der Eigentumsvorbehalt im neuen Insolvenzrecht, JZ 1995, 803-814.

Medicus, Dieter Bürgerliches Recht, 20th edition, Munich 2004.

Medicus, Dieter Allgemeiner Teil des BGB, 8th edition, Heidelberg 2002.

Mittenzwei, Ingo Gutgläubiger Erwerb gebrauchter Kraftfahrzeuge bei Handeln unter fremdem Namen, NJW 1986, 2472-2475.

Müller-Katzenburg, Astrid Besitz- und Eigentumssituationen bei gestohlenen und sonst abhanden gekommenen Kunstwerken, NJW 1999, 2551-2558.

Musielak, Hans-Joachim Eigentumserwerb an beweglichen Sachen nach § 932 ff., JuS 1992, 713-723.

Nierwetberg, Rüdiger Rechtsposition von Lieferant und Produzent nach Verarbeitung im verlängerten Eigentumsvorbehalt, NJW 1983, 2235-2236.

Ohly, Ansgar	Geistiges Eigentum?, JZ 2003, 545-554.
Olzen, Dirk	Zur Geschichte des gutgläubigen Erwerbs, Jura 1990, 505-510.
Olzen, Dirk	Die geschichtliche Entwicklung des zivilrechtlichen Eigentumsbegriffs, JuS 1984, 328-335.
Palandt, Otto (Hrsg.)	Bürgerliches Gesetzbuch, 64th edition, Munich 2005.
Pape, Gerhard / Uhlenbruck, Wilhelm	Insolvenzrecht, Munich 2002.
Picker, Eduard	Gutgläubiger Erwerb und Bereicherungsausgleich im Dreipersonenverhältnis, NJW 1974, 1790-1797.
Picker, Eduard	Mittelbarer Besitz, Nebenbesitz und Eigentumsvermutung in ihrer Bedeutung für den Gutglaubenserwerb, AcP 188 (1988), 511-571.
Rebe, Bernd	Zur Ausgleichsfunktion von § 935 zwischen Vertrauensschutz und Eigentümerinteressen beim gutgläubigen Mobiliarerwerb, AcP 173 (1973), 186-202.
Rebmann, Kurt / Säcker, Franz-Jürgen / Rixecker, Roland (eds.)	Münchener Kommentar zum Bürgerlichen Gesetzbuch, Band VI, Sachenrecht, 4th edition, Munich 2004. Cited as *Author* in: MünchKomm BGB4 VI.
Rebmann, Kurt / Säcker, Franz-Jürgen / Rixecker, Roland (eds.)	Münchener Kommentar zum Bürgerlichen Gesetzbuch, Band III, Schuldrecht – Besonderer Teil I, 4th edition, Munich 2004. Cited as *Author* in: MünchKomm BGB4 III.
Rebmann, Kurt / Säcker, Franz-Jürgen / Rixecker, Roland (eds.)	Münchener Kommentar zum Bürgerlichen Gesetzbuch, Band I, Allgemeiner Teil I, 4th edition, Munich 2001. Cited as *Author* in: MünchKomm BGB4 I.
Reichsjustizamt (ed.)	Motive zu dem Entwurf eines Bürgerlichen Gesetzbuchs, Band 3 Sachenrecht, Berlin et al. 1888, reprint 1997.
Reichsjustizamt (ed.)	Protokolle der Kommission für die zweite Lesung des Entwurfs des BGB, Band 3 Sachenrecht, Berlin et al. 1899, reprint 1997.
Schmidt, Karsten	Rechtsprechungsübersicht, JuS 1995, 1193-1194.
Schmidt, Karsten	Rechtsprechungsübersicht, JuS 1996, 458-459.
Schmidt, Karsten	Rechtsprechungsübersicht, JuS 1993, 868-869.

Schnauder, Franz	Sachen- und wertpapierrechtliche Wirkungen der kaufmännischen Traditionspapiere, NJW 1991, 1642-1649.
Schubert, Werner	Die Entstehung der Vorschriften des BGB über Besitz und Eigentumsübertragung: ein Beitrag zur Geschichte des BGB, Berlin 1966.
Schulze, Götz / Kienle, Florian	Der Kauf unter Eigentumsvorbehalt – Eine Kehrtwende des Gesetzgebers?, NJW 2002, 2842-2844.
Schulze, Rainer / Dörner, Heinrich	Bürgerliches Gesetzbuch: Handkommentar, 3rd edition, Baden-Baden 2003. Cited as: Hk-BGB/Bearbeiter.
Schwab, Karl-Heinz Prütting, Hanns	Sachenrecht: ein Studienbuch, 31st edition, Munich 2003.
Sontis, Johannes	Strukturelle Betrachtungen zum Eigentumsbegriff, in liber amoricum Karl Larenz, edited by Gotthard Paulus et al., Munich 1973, 981-1002.
Stadler, Astrid	Gestaltungsfreiheit und Verkehrsschutz durch Abstraktion: eine rechtsvergleichende Studie zur abstrakten und kausalen Gestaltung rechtsgeschäftlicher Zuwendungen anhand des deutschen, schweizerischen, österreichischen, französischen und US-amerikanischen Rechts, Tübingen 1996.
Staudinger, J. von (ed.)	Kommentar zum Bürgerlichen Gesetzbuch mit Einführungsgesetz und Nebengesetzen. Recht der Schuldverhältnisse, Zweites Buch, Besonderer Teil, § 812 - § 820. Revised edition 1999, Berlin 1999. Cited as Staudinger/*Author* (1999).
Staudinger, J. von (ed.)	Kommentar zum Bürgerlichen Gesetzbuch mit Einführungsgesetz und Nebengesetzen. Zweites Buch, Recht der Schuldverhältnisse, § 433 - § 487. Revised edition 2004, Berlin 2004. Cited as Staudinger/*Author* (2004).
Staudinger, J. von (ed.)	Kommentar zum Bürgerlichen Gesetzbuch mit Einführungsgesetz und Nebengesetzen. Erstes Buch, Allgemeiner Teil, § 90 - § 133. Revised edition 2004, Berlin 2004. Cited as Staudinger/*Author* (2004).

Staudinger, J. von (ed.)	Kommentar zum Bürgerlichen Gesetzbuch mit Einführungsgesetz und Nebengesetzen. Erstes Buch, Allgemeiner Teil 4, § 134 - § 163. Revised edition 2000, Berlin 2000. Cited as Staudinger/*Author* (2000).
Staudinger, J. von (ed.)	Kommentar zum Bürgerlichen Gesetzbuch mit Einführungsgesetz und Nebengesetzen. Drittes Buch, Sachenrecht, § 854 - § 883. Revised edition 2000, Berlin 2000. Cited as Staudinger/*Author* (2003).
Staudinger, J. von (ed.)	Kommentar zum Bürgerlichen Gesetzbuch mit Einführungsgesetz und Nebengesetzen. Drittes Buch, Sachenrecht, § 925 - § 984. Neubearbeitung 2004, Berlin 2000. Cited as Staudinger/*Author* (2004).
Stürner, Rolf	Der hundertste Geburstag des BGB – nationale Kodifikation im Greisenalter, JZ 1996, 741-752.
Taupitz, Jochen	Der deliktsrechtliche Schutz des menschlichen Körpers, NJW 1995, 745-752.
Thorn, Karsten	Mobiliarerwerb vom Nichtberechtigten: Neue Entwicklungen in rechtsvergleichender Perspektive, ZEuP 1997, 442-474.
Tiedtke, Klaus	Die Übereignung eingelagerter Ware bei Ausstellung eines Lagerscheins, WM 1979, 1142-1153.
von Caemmerer	Übereignung durch Anweisung zur Übergabe, JZ 1963, 586-588.
Wacke, Andreas	Eigentumserwerb durch schlichten Konsens oder erst mit Übergabe? Unterschiede im Rezeptionsprozeß und ihre mögliche Überwindung, ZEuP 2000, 254-262.
Wadle, Elmar	Das Problem der fremdwirkenden Verarbeitung, JuS 1982, 477-483.
Westermann, Harm Peter (ed.)	Erman Bürgerliches Gesetzbuch: Handkommentar, 11th edition, Münster 2004. Cited as Erman*Author*.
Westermann, Harrry	Sachenrecht, 6th edition, Heidelberg 1986. Cited as *H. Westermann*, Sachenrecht.
Westermann, Harrry / Westermann, Harm Peter / Gursky, Karl-Heinz / Eickmann, Dieter	Sachenrecht (begründet von Harry Westermann), 7th edition, Heidelberg 1998. Cited as Westermann/ *Author*.
Wiegand, Wolfgang	Die Entwicklung des Sachenrechts im Verhältnis zum Schuldrecht, AcP 190 (1990), 112-138.

Wieling, Hans-Josef	Vom untergegangenen, schlafenden und aufgewachten Eigentum bei Sachverbindungen, JZ 1985, 511-518.
Wieling, Hans-Josef	Voraussetzungen, Übertragung und Schutz des mittelbaren Besitzes, AcP 184 (1984), 439-464.
Wieling, Hans-Josef	Sachenrecht, 4th edition, Berlin 2001.
Witt, Carl-Heinz	Die Rechtsfigur des Besitzdieners im Widerstreit zwischen Bestands- und Verkehrsschutz, AcP 201 (2001), 165-201.
Wolf, Christian	Übertriebener Verkehrsschutz, JZ 1997, 1087-1094.
Wolff, Martin / Raiser, Ludwig	Sachenrecht: ein Lehrbuch, 10th revised edition, Tübingen 1957.
Zeranski, Dirk	Prinzipien und Systematik des gutgläubigen Erwerbs beweglicher Sachen, JuS 2002, 340-348.
Zeranski, Dirk	Eigentümer und Vorbehaltskäufer im Widerstreit um die Vorbehaltsware, AcP 203 (2003), 693-726.

Part I: Basic information on property law

§ 1. The Notion of Ownership and Other Property Rights

1. The Source of Property Law

The main source of German private law may be found in the '*Bürgerliches Gesetzbuch*' (BGB[1]), the German Civil Code. Enacted in 1896, it became effective on January 1, 1900. Adopting the pandectist system[2] (*Pandektensystem*) the Civil Code is divided into five books (*Bücher*): General Part (*Allgemeiner Teil*), Law of Obligations (*Schuldrecht*), Property Law (*Sachenrecht*), Family Law (*Familienrecht*) and Law of succession (*Erbrecht*).
Property law is the subject of the Third Book called *Sachenrecht* (literally: law of things). The Third Book contains the rules on the types, formation, transfer and protection of property rights (§§ 856-1296). Relevant provisions are also contained in the First Book of the Civil Code, titled *Allgemeiner Teil* (General Part), which contains a number of important definitions, such as the definition of 'things,' 'animals' or 'component parts.'
At first glance the structure of the Third Book of the Civil Code appears to be impenetrable,[3] as it, despite the substantial differences between movables and immovables, sets out the rules for both together within one book. First it addresses rules equally applicable to movables and immovables: the law of possession, the concept of ownership and the protection of ownership. Other rules are addressed in separate sections (or subsections) for movables and immovables, respectively: the formation, transfer, and repeal of property rights as well as the catalogue of other types of property rights. For example, section 3 subsection 2 is titled 'Acquisition and Repeal of Ownership in Immovable Property,' while section 3 subsection 3 is titled 'Acquisition and Repeal of Ownership in Movable Property.'
Although the Civil Code has undergone considerable changes since its enactment, there have been very few amendments to the Civil Code affecting property law. One of the very few relevant amendments was the introduction of a new section clarifying that animals are not things (*Sachen*).[4] Main developments in the area of property law are the result of judge-made law rather than legislative amendments of the Civil Code. The most important such developments are the recognition of

---

[1] Unless statted otherwise paragraphs mentioned hereinafter refer to the German Civil Code (BGB).

[2] *Rinne* in: MünchKomm BGB[4] VI, Introduction, no. 1.

[3] *Rinne* in: MünchKomm BGB[4] VI, Introduction, no. 2.

[4] This Act of August 20, 1990, BGBl 1990 I 1762 is rather of a symbolic nature, as despite the clarification that animals are not ‚things' it has also stated, that they are to be treated as things are, unless otherwise provided for, cf. *§ 3 I a)*.

two new concepts: the equitable interest (*Anwartschaftsrecht*) and the fiduciary transfer *(Sicherungseigentum)*. Neither of these two concepts have yet found express regulation in the Civil Code.

Further rules of property law can be found outside of the Civil Code in statutes addressing specific issues of the law on real estate and other immovable property, such as the *Wohnungseigentumsgesetz 1951*, dealing specifically with ownership interests in apartments, the *Erbbaurechtsverordnung 1919*, dealing specifically with the right to erect a building on another's property. As both acts do not concern the law of movables, they need not be dealt with in the present context. A further specific act on property law is the *Gesetz über Rechte an eingetragenen Schiffen und Schifsbauwerken 1940*, dealing with the law of registered ships and ship yards (*cf. § 4 6*).

2. The Concept of a Separate Law of Property

The structure of the Civil Code is based on the idea of a clear-cut distinction between the law of obligations *(Schuldrecht)* and the law of property *(Sachenrecht)*.[5] Evidence of this conceptual separation can be found in the treatment of contracts obliging a person to transfer property. While older continental codifications classified a contract obliging a person to transfer property as a mere prerequisite to the actual transfer and, accordingly, addresses these contracts in the context of property law,[6] the Civil Code treats such contracts as distinct and separate from the actual transfer and, accordingly, addresses such contracts in the context of contract law. Thus formation and transformation of property rights in the Civil Code are completely separated from the contract as their underlying economic justification.[7] This general principle does not only guide the structure of the code, but also reappears in the so-called '*Abstraktionsprinzip*'[8], which is one of the most important concepts of German property law.[9]

The strict distinction between the law of property and the law of obligations corresponds to the distinction between absolute rights and relative rights. While both are subjective rights, *i.e.*, a legal power conferred to an individual person,[10]

---

[5] Staudinger/*Wiegand* (2004), Introduction to § 929 no. 15; *Brehm/Berger*, Sachenrecht (2000), no. 1.4.; *Wiegand*, AcP 190 (1990), 113 ff.

[6] Cf. the third part of the Austrian Civil Code (ABGB), which contains both provisions of inheritance law and the law of obligations under the heading ‚*Sachenrecht*'; also compare the heading of § 711 French Code Civil ‚*des differentes manières dont on acquiert la propriété*'.

[7] Motive III 1.

[8] *Cf. infra 3. e).*

[9] *Wiegand*, AcP 190 (1990), 113, 120; see also *Stadler*, Gestaltungsfreiheit und Verkehrsschutz durch Abstraktion (1996), 98 ff.

[10] *Baur/Stürner*, Sachenrecht[17], § 2 no. 2.

they differ in their nature. An absolute right is effective against every other person and protects against all unlawful interference from whomsoever. A relative right, on the other hand, only grants a restricted right against a certain other person.[11]
Property rights, the so-called rights *in rem*, are absolute rights. Their substance is an absolute and direct power of a person over a thing.[12] A consequence of this characterization as a direct power is that no other person is party to this legal relationship.[13]
The law of property and the law of obligations serve different purposes: Obligatory rights, often characterized as a 'legal tie' (*rechtliches Band*) between two persons, are relative rights (cf. § 241), according to which a debtor is obliged to perform to the creditor. The content of obligatory rights are determined by the parties. They primarily affect the involved parties. Even though a change of one or both of the parties to the obligation is possible – and provided for by the rules on assignment and assumption of indebtedness, respectively – a change of parties is rather the exception than the rule. Accordingly, a party who takes over the duties of an obligatory right is expected to inform itself of the existence and the contents of such obligatory right (cf. § 404).
By contrast one of the main purposes of property law is to enable the circulation of goods. Unlike the legal tie between a debtor and a creditor, the legal bond between a person and a thing, *i.e.* a property right, is designed to be transferred. This distinct function of property law, in turn, generates a particular demand for marketability. The characteristics of property law, such as the restriction to certain statutorily defined types of property rights and the concept of absolute rights, facilitate this marketability.
The strict separation of relative and absolute rights, however, cannot always be maintained.[14] For the violation of an absolute right creates a relative right against the violator. This relative right can neither be separated from the right *in rem*, nor can it be disposed of separately. Rather, it forms an integral part of the absolute right.[15] The distinction has been weakened in another manner as well. A number

---

[11] Therefore absolute rights are not restricted to property law, but may also be found in the context of intellectual property law as in family and inheritance law.

[12] *Rinne* in: MünchKomm BGB[4] VI, Introduction, no. 4. This generally accepted concept, however, is critisized by *Hadding*, JZ 1986, 926, 927, because the legal order always concerns the rules on interaction between human beings. Accordingly also property rights actually concern the delimitation of power between fellow citizens.

[13] This even holds true for restricted rights *in rem*: in case of conflict between the owner and the holder of the restricted property right, the owner cannot unilaterally terminate the restricted property right. Similarly co-ownership cannot be terminated unilaterally but has to be but has to be dissolved according to the statutory rules, cf. *Brehm/Berger*, Sachenrecht (2000), no. 1.10.

[14] Cf. *Baur/Stürner*, Sachenrecht[17], § 2 no. 3 f.

[15] *Mager*, AcP 193 (1993), 69, 72 ff. The question whether the claim for delivery arising from ownership may be assigned separately is a matter of dispute, cf. *Baur/Stürner*, Sachenrecht[17], § 11 no. 44 and *§ 5 4 c)*.

of important relative rights have been granted distinct attributes of rights *in rem*[16] and thereby are afforded a degree of protection that is similar, or at least comparable, to rights *in rem*. Strengthened to such an extent these relative rights are referred to as rights *quasi-in rem* (*quasi-dingliche Rechte*). The law of tenancy is one area where such a development has taken place (*cf. § 2 4 a*).

3. General Principles of Property Law

One of the most important principles of German property law has already been mentioned above: the restriction of rights *in rem* to certain legally defined types (the so-called *numerus clausus*). In addition there are four other basic principles, which represent the corner stones of German property law. These are the principle of absolute effect, publicity, specificity and the so-called *Abstraktionsprinzip*. These five principles are closely connected to each other and partly even overlap. A clear-cut distinction therefore is not always possible.[17]

a) Exclusivity

The concept of the principle of exclusivity, also-called the *numerus clausus* of rights *in rem*, is a restriction of available types of rights *in rem* to those types set out by statute law. This is even more clearly described by the alternative term restriction of types (*Typenzwang*).[18]
The Civil Code provides for a limited number – in fact six different types – of property rights. The parties may choose between these types of property rights explicitly set out. But they may neither agree on new types nor mix those provided for, as this would contradict the so-called 'definition of types' (*Typenfixierung*).[19] Mandatory provisions set our the rights and duties following from a chosen type as well as the content. The freedom of determination (*Inhaltsfreiheit*) and the freedom to create legal relationships (*inhaltliche Gestaltungsfreiheit*), which is a characteristic of the law of obligations, therefore is to a great extent[20] restricted in property law.[21]
As mentioned above this restriction serves the marketability of property rights. But it is also serves the protection of ownership as the most valuable (property)

---

[16] *Canaris*, FS Flume (1978), 371, 372.
[17] *Rinne* in: MünchKomm BGB⁴ VI, Introduction, no. 9.
[18] *Baur/Stürner*, Sachenrecht[17], § 1 no. 7.
[19] *Baur/Stürner*, Sachenrecht[17], § 1 no. 7.
[20] The parties, however, have the possibility to modify property rights by insertion of conditions or a time-limit, cf. *Rinne* in: MünchKomm BGB[4] VI, Introduction, no. 11.
[21] *Baur/Stürner*, Sachenrecht[17], § 1 no. 7.

right, against excessive encumbrances.[22] If encumbrance were possible without limitations, then the overarching right of ownership would perhaps deteriorate to a *nudum ius*. This protection against excessive burdens of course, first and foremost, is of importance in the context of real estate law. However, this restriction can also serve its purpose with regard to movables; for instance the legal framework of securities by means of fiduciary transfer of ownership do serve to balance the interest of the creditor in the security (*i.e.* the possibility of realization of the securities furnished) against the protection of the debtor (*i.e.* the concerning in particular the modalities of realization and enforcement).[23]
A further justification for the restriction to a limited number of property rights may be found in the characterisation of rights *in rem* as absolute rights, that is their impact on third parties. If everybody is bound to respect absolute rights, it is a prerequisite that everybody is in the position to make out the content of that right. Of course, such absolute protection should only be granted as far as the need for such far-reaching protection is acknowledged by the legal order. Accordingly, it cannot be left to the disposition of the individual parties to create rights *in rem* of various scopes and content.[24]
The clarity of form reached by the *numerus clausus* at the same time prevents the emergence of an impenetrable variety of rights *in rem* and thereby serves the interest of the community in legal clarity.[25] For it dispenses the transferee of property rights to scrutinize the authority of the transferor and the content of the property right in question in every single legal transaction. A scrutiny which is almost impossible, as the transferee does not have access to the state of affairs of the transferor.[26] The fluency and safety of legal transactions is further promoted by the straightforwardness: the parties don't have to negotiate in detail which rights and duties are transferred in every single legal transaction, but instead can rely on the enumerated types of property rights set out by law.[27] This function of the *numerus clausus* is of utmost importance in the context of movables.[28]
Despite the general acceptance of the principle of *numerus clausus*[29] two new types of rights *in rem*, or *quasi rights in rem*[30] respectively, have been acknowledged both by legal doctrine and by the judicature: first, the credit

---

[22] Cf. *Brehm/Berger*, Sachenrecht (2000), no. 1.36.
[23] *Baur/Stürner*, Sachenrecht[17], § 56 no. 1.
[24] *Baur/Stürner*, Sachenrecht[17], § 1 no. 11; cf. Motive III 3.
[25] *Brehm/Berger*, Sachenrecht (2000), no. 5.2.
[26] Cf. *Baur/Stürner*, Sachenrecht[17], § 1 no. 12.
[27] *Baur/Stürner*, Sachenrecht[17], § 1 no. 9.
[28] *Baur/Stürner*, Sachenrecht[17], § 49 no. 4.
[29] But cf. *Schubert*, Die Entstehung der Vorschriften des BGB über Besitz und Eigentumsübertragung (1966), 163, who demonstrates that both the first and the second commission have rejected a prohibition of security by transfer of title.
[30] *Baur/Stürner*, Sachenrecht[17], § 3 no. 47.

security by transfer of ownership and second, equitable interests (cf. *infra § 8*). These new types correspond to the demand of modern economy for flexible lending arrangements and corresponding flexible security arrangements. In addition to this pragmatic argument this development is also justified by the argument, that the *numerus clausus* merely addresses the individual parties, but does not hinder legal developments as such.[31]

b) Absolute Effect

Property rights have absolute effect, *i.e.* they can be invoked against whoever interferes with the exclusive enjoyment of property rights. This categorization as absolute depicts the main criterion to distinguish them from mere obligatory rights, namely their effect against third parties.

This absolute effect is mirrored by the comprehensive protection of rights *in rem*. First and foremost the owner is protected against dispossession by the *rei vindicatio*. Any other interference with his ownership may be remedied by an action for abatement of nuisance or a petition for a restraining order (*actio negatoria*). As these remedies emanate from the right of ownership, both actions will be granted independently of whether or not the violator is to be blamed for his act. In case the property is culpably damaged the owner, in addition, may claim damages under tort law provision (§ 823 section 1).

The scope of this absolute protection is widened to include holders of other property rights according to the respective scope of that property right.[32] For instance both the *rei vindicatio* and the *actio negatoria* are granted not only to the owner but also to the usufructuary (§ 1065) and to the pledgee of a movable (§ 1227). Such other property rights constitute '*other rights*' in the meaning of § 823 and therefore are evenly protected by tort law (cf. *infra 7.*).

A further aspect of the nature of rights *in rem* as absolute is that the right of ownership is not considered to be a bundle of various separate rights, but is indivisible.[33] A fragmentation of ownership cannot even be reached by express agreement. It is therefore impossible to provide that one person is to be regarded as owner in respect to one category of persons, while a second person exercises the rights against another category of people. This indivisibility is further secured by the restraint on disposition under § 137. This provision prevents the restriction of the right to dispose of a right *in rem* by contractual agreement. However, this rule has not remained without exceptions. Two are even expressly provided for in the Civil Code: first, the priority note in the land register, second, the relative *pactum de non alienando*. In addition, also the division of fiduciary property into

---

[31] Cf. *Canaris*, FS Flume (1978), 371, 376.
[32] *Baur/Stürner*, Sachenrecht[17], § 4 no. 6.
[33] *Baur/Stürner*, Sachenrecht[17], § 4 no. 7; *Wiegand*, AcP 190 (1990), 113, 117.

legal property of the security holder and economic property of the party furnishing security creditor is acknowledged.[34]

c) Publicity

The aim of the principle of publicity is to secure that rights *in rem* are apparent to third parties. The means to achieve this publicity in respect of rights *in rem* in movables is possession, while with regard to immovables this function is fulfilled by entry into the land register. The legislator of the Civil Code intended that, as a general rule, the possession of things as it may be perceived by the public and the underlying legal authority shall correspond. This principle that possession and ownership shall correspond at the same time serves as a basis for the presumption of ownership in § 1006.[35]

However, in the law on movables so many exceptions from the principle of publicity may be found that the rule has lost some of its strength.[36] The reason for this development is both the acceptance of transfer of ownership without (public) transfer of possession and the growing importance of contractual relationships that grant a non-owner a right of possession. Thus from the mere fact that a person lawfully possesses a thing, it does no longer necessarily follow that this possessor is entitled to hold such possession by a right *in rem* (cf. *infra § 2 2. c*).

Having already mentioned the existence of various exceptions to the principle of publicity with regard to movables, it has to be stated that the principle of publicity can only claim limited authority.[37] Exceptions to the rule may in particular be found in § 930 ff. on the so-called substitutes for *traditio* (*Übergabesurrogate*) as well as in the rules on *ex lege* acquisition of rights *in rem*. This latter exception for instance applies in case of acquisition of property by the heir, where transfer is reduced to a *traditio ficta* (cf. § 857). In addition the concepts both of credit securities by fiduciary transfer of ownership developed *praeter legem* and of equitable interest lack adherence to the principle of publicity.[38] Despite these numerous exceptions and their practical importance the principle of publicity is still regarded as a basic principle of German property law.

---

[34] *Baur/Stürner*, Sachenrecht[17], § 4 no. 7. This inconsistency is criticised by *Olzen*, JuS 1984, 328, 330 and 335.

[35] In fact the presumption of ownership according to § 1006 only constitutes the presumption, that transfer of possession and acquisition of title coincide, but not that the possessor who does not claim to have acquired property at the time of transfer of possession is the owner, cf. *Rebe*, AcP 173 (1973), 186, 194.

[36] *Rinne* in: MünchKomm BGB[4] VI, Introduction, no. 21.

[37] *Brehm/Berger*, Sachenrecht (2000), no. 1.43.

[38] *Baur/Stürner*, Sachenrecht[17], § 4 no. 10.

The means to implement the principle of publicity with regard to movables[39] is the concept of the principle of *traditio* (*Traditionsprinzip*). According to this *Traditionsprinzip* the acquisition of a right *in rem* must become apparent by an actual change of physical control. Accordingly, the rules on transfer of title in movables in general require publicity of the transfer, *i.e.* the actual transfer of physical control over the asset involved (*traditio*). Both the transfer of ownership in movables according to § 929 and the acquisition of pledge according to § 1205 may serve as an example. Both require the actual transfer of physical control.
The principle of tradition according to the prevailing opinion serves two purposes: first, it makes the change of rights *in rem* apparent for the public.[40] Second, it secures the genuineness of the transfer of property. This additional aspect is also referred to as function of reliability (*Seriositätsfunktion*).

d) Specificity

The principle of specificity (*Bestimmtheitsgrundsatz*) can similarly be understood as a consequence of the principle of publicity. Its aim is to contribute to clarity and certainty with respect to rights *in rem*.[41]
As it is a necessary prerequisite for the duty of everybody to respect the absolute rights of others (absolute effect) that everyone has knowledge of this duty, it must be apparent which things are the subject of such property rights. Therefore every property right has to relate to a specific thing. The exact determination of the subject of property rights further is a precondition for the exercise of the absolute power over a thing, as it is impossible to exercise direct power over things only specified by quantity or kind.
According to this principle of specificity rights *in rem* can only be established with regard to certain isolated things. In order to comply with the principle of specificity every real agreement must determine which goods precisely are covered by a certain legal transaction. Because each thing is the subject of a separate right of ownership and accordingly a separate real agreement, it follows that in case of a transfer of aggregate things the requirements for the transfer have to be complied with in regard to every single thing. This requirement is only fulfilled if it is apparent for both the parties to the contract as well as for third parties which movables have been the subject of a new allocation of rights *in rem*.[42]

---

39 As far as rights in immovables are concerned the *traditio* is replaced by an entry into the land register (cf. § 873 and § 925).
40 Cf. *Brehm/Berger*, Sachenrecht (2000), no. 26.12.
41 *Baur/Stürner*, Sachenrecht[17], § 4 no. 17.
42 Westermann/*Westermann*, Sachenrecht[7] I, § 3 II 1; also compare *Feuerborn*, ZIP 2001, 600, 602.

Accordingly the transfer of a business entity cannot be effected *uno acto*, but instead has to follow the rules for the respective separate components, the rules on transfer of ownership in immovables (§ 873, § 925) or movables (§ 929 ff.) respectively. In case of generic goods it must be precisely determined which individual assets are covered. The same applies in case of aggregate things, such as a stock of merchandise, which has to be determinable in its contents.[43] Accordingly it would violate the principle of specificity to create a general mortgage or grant a fiduciary transfer of ownership with respect to an 'entire property'. However, also the principle of specificity has been alleviated, in particular as far as the developments of securities by fiduciary transfer of ownership and the (extended) reservation of title are concerned (cf. *infra § 13 3.*).[44]

As far as the transfer of title requires actual *traditio*, that is transfer of physical control, the requirement of specificity will in general not require any particular precautions. It is impossible to transfer physical control over unspecified things.[45] However, in case the transfer of title is not accompanied by a factual transfer of direct possession, then the real agreement effecting the transfer requires that the thing covered by this agreement is specified.

e) Abstract Nature of Rights *in rem*

The principle of the abstract nature of rights *in rem* (*Abstraktionsprinzip*) goes back to *Friedrich von Savigny* and his theory of the real agreement.[46] It is based on the division of the act of acquisition of ownership into two separate legal acts, first, the underlying legal act that obliges the transferor to transfer ownership and second, the subsequent legal act which effectuates the transfer. The former is referred to as obligatory act (*Verpflichtungsgeschäft*), the latter as real agreement (*Verfügungsgeschäft*). This distinction itself is referred to as principle of division (*Trennungsgrundsatz*).

Based on this principle of division, the *Abstraktionsprinzip* declares that the validity of the real agreement as a rule is independent of the validity of the underlying obligatory act. Transfer of ownership under German law accordingly does not require any *iusta causa traditionis*.[47] Even if the real agreement lacks an economic justification, because the obligatory act is invalid, the transfer is still

---

[43] Cf. BGH JZ 1988, 471.

[44] Cf. *Baur/Stürner*, Sachenrecht[17], § 4 no. 19.

[45] Staudinger/*Wiegand* (2004), § 929 no. 12.

[46] Staudinger/*Seiler* (2000), Introduction to property law, no. 49.

[47] This requirement is for example contained in § 424 Austrian ABGB. For a similar requirement compare the *cause licite* under art. 1108 French Code Civile; for further details see *Brehm/Berger*, Sachenrecht (2000), no. 1.20 ff.

held to be valid. The transferee has acquired ownership, but due to the lack of an economic justification the transfer has to be reversed. Different from a causal system it will though not be resolved by revindication, but instead by recourse to the law of unjustified enrichment (§ 812 ff.).[48]

This formal independence (*äußere Abstraktion*), that is the independence of obligatory agreement and real agreement is further completed by the so-called material independence (*innere Abstraktion*)[49]. Its substance is that the sole subject of the real agreement is the transfer of ownership and apart from this is not considered to serve any further purpose.[50] This material independence at the same time is a major justification for the formal independence: because the real agreement does not serve any outside purpose it will not be affected by any defects of the parties' intentions forming the obligatory agreement. The violation of *boni mores* may serve as an example. As the real agreement is neutral, it cannot be invalidated by the violation of *boni mores* by the contractual agreement. Despite some exceptions (*cf. § 4 3 c*) legal doctrine and judicature as a general rule remain faithful to the *Abstraktionsprinzip*.[51]

4. Notion of ownership

According to the concept of the legislator ownership is the most comprehensive and all-embracing property right. A legal definition of the notion of ownership is contained in § 903.

> **§ 903 BGB [Powers of the Owner]**
>
> (1) The owner of a thing may, to the extent that it is not contrary to the law or the rights of third parties, deal with the thing as he pleases and exclude others from any interference.

The concept of a comprehensive right at the same time rejects the idea of property as a bundle of separate rights.[52] It is therefore impossible to enumerate the different powers comprised in the right of ownership. Yet, from a practical perspective the two most important legal powers of the owner of a thing are first, the right to make (economic) use and to realize the value by legal transaction, and second, to either exclude any third party from its use or to share its use. From this all-embracing power to dispose of one's goods particular powers can be 'split apart' and granted to other parties as so-called restricted property rights

---

[48] *Cf. infra b) aa.*

[49] This distinction was first elaborated on by *Jahr*, AcP 168 (1968), 9, 16 ff.

[50] This material independence is comparable to an abstract promise creating an independant obligation (*abstraktes Schuldversprechen*).

[51] Cf. *Wiegand*, AcP 190 (1990), 113, 125.

[52] For details see *Sontis*, in FS Larenz (1973), 981, 993.

(*beschränkt dingliche Rechte*). However, this possibility does not affect the nature of ownership as an all-embracing property right, as such restricted property rights can neither be established permanently nor irrevocably.[53]
The concept of ownership is a result of the strong influence of *Friedrich von Savigny*:[54] ownership is not merely a concept to allocate property to different members of society, but rather conceived as a civil liberty.[55] Therefore the structure of the right of ownership at the same time is a declaration of rejection of prior concepts of divided ownership. This function of a guarantee of civil liberties explains the by tradition close connection between the notion of ownership comprised in § 903 BGB, on the one hand, and art. 14 of the Basic Law, the German Constitutional Act (*Grundgesetz*), on the other hand.[56] In line with the judicature of the Federal Constitutional Court the fundamental right of ownership has the function to guarantee to each individual an area of freedom of economic disposition and thereby allow him to independently take responsibility for his lead of life.[57]

> **Article 14 GG [Property, Inheritance, Expropriation]**
>
> (1) Property and the right of inheritance shall be guaranteed. Their content and limits shall be defined by the laws.
>
> (2) Property entails obligations. Its use shall also serve the public good.
>
> (3) Expropriation shall only be permissible for the public good. It may only be ordered by or pursuant to a law that determines the nature and extent of compensation. Such compensation shall be determined by establishing an equitable balance between the public interest and the interests of those affected. In case of dispute respecting the amount of compensation, recourse may be had to the ordinary courts.

Although the notion of ownership of the Basic Law is different from the underlying concept of ownership of the Civil Code – and in particular has been extended far beyond the scope of property in the meaning of § 903 BGB by the judicature of the Federal Constitutional Court – yet it shows that the conflict between private autonomy or freedom of ownership and the necessary and permissible restrictions of the power of ownership cannot be resolved by private law alone. It must be decided by reference to the Basic Law.

---

[53] *Brehm/Berger*, Sachenrecht (2000), no. 5.8.
[54] *Brehm/Berger*, Sachenrecht (2000), no. 1.2.
[55] Cf. *Brehm/Berger*, Sachenrecht (2000), no. 5.4.
[56] Cf. *Georgiades*, FS Sontis (1977), 149, 156 ff.; *Sontis*, in FS Larenz (1973), 981, 999 f.; *Olzen*, JuS 1984, 328 ff.
[57] BVerfGE 68, 193, 222.

Provisions on the scope and substance of the right of ownership as of other property rights and their restrictions respectively may not only be found within private law but – steadily growing in numbers – also in the area of public law.[58] Rules of public law pertaining to property law primarily regulate matters such as expropriation or building permissions. Thus they primarily concern the law of immovable property, while the conflicting interest of owners and third parties concerning movable property are far less severe.[59] Notwithstanding this practical differences, both the guarantee of the institution of ownership provided for by art. 14 GG as well as the individual guarantee of ownership as a fundamental freedom do also comprise movable property. They are in particular often referred to in the discussion of *bona fide*-acquisition and acquisitive prescription.[60] Similarly do the restrictions of ownership developed in the context of immovable property apply to movables,[61] as well as the protection provided by art. 14 section 3 GG against expropriation also includes movables.[62]
A further important restriction of the all-embracing power of ownership under § 903 BGB results from the function of the concept of ownership (as of other property rights) to promote peace. Every holder of a property right is obliged to respect the rights of others. Further he may not exercise his power in an unlawful fashion. This is of particular importance in the area of neighbour law, but also has some relevancy in respect of movable goods.

5. Protection of Ownership

a) Claims Arising From Property Law

The privileges of the owner, namely to enjoy quiet possession of the property, to use it without interference and to gain the profits or fruits, are mirrored by the different measures of protection arising from property law, which are granted to the owner: the claim to recover property, the right to petition for a restraining order and the right to claim abatement of a nuisance. These claims serve the comprehensive protection of absolute property rights and are inseparable parts of these property rights.[63] The right to enjoy the profits or fruits of ownership are in

---

[58] *Baur/Stürner*, Sachenrecht[17], § 1 no. 1.
[59] *Baur/Stürner*, Sachenrecht[17], § 50 no. 2.
[60] Cf. *Baldus* in: MünchKomm BGB[4] VI, § 937 no. 43 and *Quack* in: MünchKomm BGB[4] VI, § 932 no. 2.
[61] BVerfGE 30, 351; BGH NJW 1965, 1080, 1082.
[62] The possibility of expropriation of movables is provided for in § 2 *Bundesleistungsgesetz*. The requirements are that the movable is necessary in the public interest and the need cannot be met, or not timely or only with disproportionate costs.
[63] *Brehm/Berger*, Sachenrecht (2000), no. 1.13.

addition protected by a claim for compensation arising out of the owner-possessor-relationship (*Eigentümer-Besitzer-Verhältnis*), an obligatory right in case a third party makes use of the property without authorization.
These means of protection particularly designed for property rights, *rei vindicatio*, *actio negatoria* and the claim for compensation arising from the owner-possessor-relationship are further completed by other remedies, which are not by nature particular to property law. Yet, without them comprehensive protection of property rights could not be guaranteed. They comprise claims for damages, claims *ex* unjustified enrichment and the protection of the owner in case of default or insolvency of the possessor.

aa) Revindication

The right to (re-)claim property is provided for by § 985.

§ 985 BGB [Claim for Delivery]

The owner can demand from the possessor the delivery of the thing.
According to § 985 the dispossessed owner may claim recovery of the thing from the possessor. The aim of the claim is to recover property in the current condition. Thus the possessor has to (re-)transfer possession to the owner. In case the opponent party is merely an indirect possessor the owner may according to the prevailing opinion[64] either claim delivery or transfer of indirect possession.[65] The subsequent provisions set out that recovery may only be claimed from an unjustified possessor.[66] Therefore the possessor may oppose to the claim for recovery if he is entitled to possession.
Such a right to retain possession may arise from either a restricted property right or be of a merely obligatory nature. It will further suffice to reject the claim, if the direct possessor can derive his right from another person, who has a right of possession against the owner and is authorized to entrust possession to a third party. This for example may be the case if the lessee lets the good to a sub-lessee.
Revindication can only be instituted against the current possessor. In case the possessor looses possession the claim of the owner to revindicate the thing from that (former) possessor ceases, whether or not the possessor is to blame for the loss of possession. For he in fact is unable to provide for recovery. As far as the further requirements of § 989, § 990 or § 992 are met, the claim for revindication is substituted by a claim for damages. Of course, the owner can also turn to the new possessor.

---

[64] BGHZ 2, 164, 166; BGHZ 12, 380, 397; BGHZ 53, 29.
[65] Of other opinion *Baur/Stürner*, Sachenrecht[17], § 11 no. 41 ff., who deny a claim for recovery in respect of the indirect possessor.
[66] *Baur/Stürner*, Sachenrecht[17], § 11 no. 24.

The claim for recovery under § 985 neither comprises a right to self-help nor a right to resort to force (cf. § 859). If the possessor is unwilling to deliver the property to the owner the owner will have to call for the assistance of the court. The judgment granted then gives the right to have the claim for recovery enforced according to § 894 ZPO.[67] In case the disposal of the cause of action would be belated the owner can also apply for an interim injunction. On the basis of such interim injunction the court's officer may then take possession of the goods and hand them over to the owner (§ 883 ZPO).
The claim for recovery *in rem* is not only granted to the owner, but by means of reference also to other holders of property rights, who by virtue of their property right have a right to possession, such as the pledgee of a movable (§ 1227).

bb) Actio Negatoria

The *actio negatoria* is a restraining order. It provides the owner with a remedy against all unlawful inferences with his property other than deprivation or retention of possession (both situations covered by the *rei vindicatio*, cf. *supra aa*).[68] The scope of protection of § 1004 is derived from the powers of the owner under § 903. Together with the *rei vindicatio* the *actio negatoria* serves the comprehensive protection of ownership.
As far as § 985 is not applicable the owner can restrain any other interference with his authority to dispose with his property according to his own liking by a petition for an abatement order concerning existing interference or a restraining order concerning future interference. The interference may consist of an act or the continuance of nuisance. Accordingly the *actio negatoria* is only applicable as far as the interference is a human act or is at least the consequence of a human act.[69] The claim goes against the so-called violator (*Störer*), that is the person responsible for the interference.
Both orders require that the interference is unlawful. In case the owner is under a duty to tolerate the interference the *actio negatoria* is precluded (§ 1004 subsection 2). Such duty to tolerate can for example be based on the prior permission of the owner, a contract or a restricted other property right, but by exception may also find its basis directly in the law (*e.g.* assistance in state of emergency).
A person who suffers interference of ownership can demand the abatement of the nuisance if the nuisance subsists or the prolongation is impending. The protection afforded is restricted to the right to claim a *contrarius actus*, that is to abate the

---

[67] Zivilprozessordnung (Civil Procedure Rules).
[68] *Baur/Stürner*, Sachenrecht[17], § 12 no. 1.
[69] *Baur/Stürner*, Sachenrecht[17], § 12 no. 18.

source of the nuisance, but does not grant the right to claim damages concerning damage that has already occurred (*on damages cf. 5 b aa*).[70]

The claim for abatement of a nuisance is litigated by an action for affirmatory relief and has to set out the necessary measures. The judgment for affirmatory relief will in case of an act, which can be replaced by another person, be enforced according to § 887 ZPO; in case it cannot be substituted it will be enforced by coercive measures against the violator (§ 888 ZPO).

If further occurrence of nuisance is imminent the owner may petition for a restraining order. He will have to prove both his ownership and the danger of repetition. A prohibitory judgement granted will be enforced according to § 890 ZPO: further interference with the court order will be sanctioned by coercive measures.

As mentioned above one of the prerequisites of a restraining order is the danger of repetition of the nuisance. Repetition at the same time indicates that a first interference must already have taken place. Yet, the owner who fears instantaneously impending danger should not be forced to await the danger to occur. Although not covered by a literal interpretation a precautionary restraining order is granted, in case a danger has not yet occurred but is impending.[71] Instead of asserting the danger of repetition the owner will have to assert and prove that a first interference is forthcoming.

Restraining orders provided for by § 1004 are of great practical importance and are more often applied than for example the *rei vindicatio*.[72] The main application, however, is to be found in the law of immovable property, in particular in the area of neighbour law and the law of industrial property. As far as movable property is concerned the most important interference is private nuisance. Well known cases are the application for a restraining order by a producer of beverages against a competitor who refilled and resold the claimant's bottles[73] or the action of a business against some employees who had attached advertisements of the trade union to their helmets, which were the property of the business.[74]

cc) Claims for Compensation Arising from the Owner-Possessor-Relationship

The mere right to claim delivery of the goods and abatement or restraint of nuisance respectively is no sufficient protection, if the deprivation or retention of possession has caused damage to the owner which will not be compensated by the mere return of the goods. This in particular applies in case the dispossessed owner

---

[70] *Baur/Stürner*, Sachenrecht[17], § 12 no. 20.
[71] BGHZ 2, 394; BGH LM § 1004, no. 27; *Baur/Stürner*, Sachenrecht[17], § 12 no. 25.
[72] *Baur/Stürner*, Sachenrecht[17], § 12 no. 4.
[73] BGH LM § 1004 BGB no. 27.
[74] BAG AP 1980 art. 9 Basic Law no. 30.

was deprived of the fruits or profits of his property or in case the asset has been damaged or has sustained a loss of value while it has been in the custody of the person now under an obligation to return the asset.
The owner in addition to the claim for recovery of the asset (cf. *supra aa*) therefore is granted a claim for compensation arising from the so-called owner-possessor-relationship (*Eigentümer-Besitzer-Verhältnisses*). Such compensation covers damages and delivery of profits. If the possessor has incurred expenses of maintenance in the meantime, he may, as a general rule, in turn claim compensation from the owner. Of course, the claim for compensation has to fail if the possessor has a right to retain possession: in this case the further requirement of §§ 987 ff., namely the existence of a *Vindikationslage* is lacking.[75] A *Vindikationslage* only exists in case all the requirements for a *rei vindicatio* are met.
Both the extent of compensation the owner may claim from the possessor as the recompense of maintenance costs incurred the possessor may claim from the owner will of course depend on whether the possessor had a just reason to believe he was entitled to the use of the asset or whether he knew he was unauthorized.

b) Further General Means of Protection

aa) Claim for Damages

According to the provision of § 823 subsection 1 a person who, wilfully or negligently, unlawfully injures the property or other right of another is bound to compensate him for any damage arising therefrom. This general rule of tort law also protects property rights against damage. It is further established that this protection also includes the equitable interest, this equitable interest being acknowledged as '*another right*' in the meaning of § 823 subsection 1.
However, the general rules of tort law may to some extent conflict with the provisions particular tailored to property law. This conflict is resolved by the rule that both the *rei vindicatio* and the claim for compensation arising from the owner-possessor-relationship prevail over the application of tort law rules, unless property law rules explicitly refer to the latter as is the case in § 992. By contrast the *actio negatoria* does not preclude any claim for damages arising from tortious injury of property, because the *actio negatoria* only grants a right to claim abatement and restraint of further nuisance, but does not compensate for any damage that has already arisen. The compensation of such damage therefore is

[75] Established practice of the courts since BGHZ 27, 317; cf. BGHZ 34, 122, 128; BGHZ 100, 95. Then again judicature tends to apply §§ 987 ff. also to the lawful possessor. This is criticized by *Baur/Stürner*, Sachenrecht[17], § 11 no. 24 fn. 2 (with further references).

governed by the generally applicable rules of tort law. The main difference of course is that the obligation to compensate under tort law depends on the fault of the tortfeasor, whereas the property law claims do not require any fault.[76]

bb) Unjustified Enrichment

The general rules on unjustified enrichment also apply to property law relationships and may be found in § 812 ff. The basic principle is set out in § 812.

> **§ 812 BGB [General Rule]**
>
> (1) A person who obtains something by performance by another person or in another way at the expense of this person without legal cause is bound to give it up to him. The same obligation exists if the legal cause later lapses or if the result does not occur which the performance had been aimed at to produce according to the content of the legal transaction.

This general rule comes into play in case a conducted transaction lacks its underlying justification, because the underlying obligatory act is void or has been annulled.
In addition unjustified enrichment law in § 816 also provides for a rule, which is specifically designed for the context of property law. It governs the consequences of transfer of title by an unauthorized person. A further particular claim *ex* unjustified enrichment is contained in § 951 on the compensation for loss of ownership by *accessio*, *confusio* and *specificatio* (cf. *infra § 10*). As far as a compensation for interference is neither provided for by tort law nor from (impure) benevolent intervention a claim *ex* unjustified enrichment may be granted according to the general rules (cf. § 812 ff.).[77]

cc) Protection Against Possessor's Default

One of the most important characteristics of rights *in rem* is that they are secure against default and bankruptcy. Thus there are specific remedies which provide for the case that the possessor of the owner's property does not satisfy his debts and his creditors therefore – in the process of enforcing their claims against the possessor – intend to seize the owner's property. In case the creditors levy execution against the possessor the owner is granted the remedy of a third-party action against execution; in case the possessor declares bankruptcy the owner can, as a general rule, claim release from the estate. Different rules may apply to

---

[76] For details see *Armbrüster*, NJW 2003, 3087 f.
[77] Cf. LG Aachen NJW 1984, 2421 and KG Berlin NJW 1985, 1714.

specific forms of ownership, such as fiduciary ownership, where the right of the owner is restricted to a claim for segregation from estate (cf. *infra § 8*).

i) Third-party action against execution

As far as execution is imposed on the property of the owner in the course of enforcement process against the possessor, the owner can institute a third-party action against execution to protect his property rights. By virtue of this claim the owner can rebut the general presumption that all property in the possession of the debtor is owned by that debtor. In case the owner succeeds with his action the measures of execution concerning his property are declared invalid. He may recover his property.

ii) Right of Separation and Preferential Claim

The owner is further granted a specific remedy for the situation that the possessor of his property declares bankruptcy and his property is held to be part of the estate in bankruptcy. He may claim release from estate and thereby prevent that his property is realized within the insolvency proceedings against the possessor.
However, different rules apply in case an owner can only claim the formal position of ownership, which merely serves security interests, while the exclusive authority to use the property rests with the possessor. The fact that from an economic perspective the possessor would be the owner will be taken into account in the insolvency proceedings. Consequently the owner cannot claim release from estate and recovery of the asset, but merely is entitled to segregation from estate. The owner is granted preferential payment, however, if the value of the asset exceeds the amount of the unsettled debts, then the superfluous value will flow to the estate in bankruptcy (cf. *infra § 8*).

c) The Interaction of the Different Remedies

The three specific remedies granted by property law, namely *rei vindicatio*, *actio negatoria* and compensation arising from the owner-possessor-relationship are independent of each other and therefore may be cumulated. On the other hand, the relationship between the latter and in particular the law of unjustified enrichment and tort law is problematic, because the system of claims arising from the owner-possessor-relationship does have characteristics both of tort law and of unjustified enrichment law. The prevailing opinion in legal doctrine as in judicature holds

that §§ 987 ff. in general are of exclusive character, but allow exceptions in order to prevent a conflict of values.[78]
The application of tort law also is precluded as far as this would interfere with the allocation of property derived from property law rules. *Bona fide*-acquisition may serve as an example: the possibility to acquire ownership from an unauthorized person may not be rendered ineffective by granting the former owner a claim for restitution in kind against the acquirer (cf. *infra § 11 9.*).[79]
An exception from the general rule that property law prevails over tort law and the law of unjustified enrichment is also necessary in case of the specific situation that the possessor has received possession without justification, *i.e.* because the real agreement is void. Here the possessor is treated as if merely the contractual agreement were void, not the real agreement: § 812 is applicable.[80]

6. Other Property Rights in Movables

The Civil Code in §§ 1018 ff. acknowledges a number of different restricted property rights. In contrast to ownership as the all-embracing property right, they are restricted powers and exist next to the ownership with respect to the same thing.
With regard to the content of such restricted property rights the Civil Code distinguishes between two distinct groups: first, rights of enjoyment and second, rights of security and realization. In addition there is a third group of restricted property rights, the so-called rights to acquire property. As the Civil Code has not provided for them as a distinct group they are to be found at various different positions in the Code.
Next to these mentioned property rights further specific rights exist, which are not rights *in rem* in the strict sense and therefore not included in the phrase 'other property rights', but have been assimilated to rights *in rem*. They include the right of pre-emption in immovable property (§ 1094), notation in the land register (§ 883), exclusive right to appropriation of land (§ 928) and finally equitable interest, which is not provided for by the Civil Code.[81]
Of course, the main importance of such restricted property rights arises in the context of the law of immovables, whereas the law of movables only knows a very limited number of restricted rights *in rem*. There is a single right of enjoyment of another's property (usufruct) and a single security right (pledge). By contrast security by transfer of title (fiduciary transfer) and equitable interest arising from a sale with a stipulated reservation of title play an important part in

---

[78] *Baur/Stürner*, Sachenrecht[17], § 11 no. 34 with reference to BGHZ 14, 7, 8.
[79] *Baur/Stürner*, Sachenrecht[17], § 12 no. 6.
[80] *Baur/Stürner*, Sachenrecht[17], § 11 no. 38.
[81] Cf. *infra § 13*.

the law of movables. Both have not been provided for by the Civil Code, but there existence has been widely acknowledged by both judicature and legal doctrine Although it is the subject of a long-standing dispute whether or not they fall within the category of rights *in rem*, their main features should be set out subsequent to those of the (other) restricted property rights.

In this context it must be mentioned that possession is not considered to be a right *in rem*. The same holds true for other absolute rights which grant a position similar to ownership of property, but are not rights *in rem* because they concern intangible goods. Examples are the right to hold a name or intellectual property rights.[82]

Further exclusions from the rights *in rem* concern a number of so-called rights *quasi-in rem* (*quasi-dingliche Rechte*). This term describes obligatory rights which *inter alia* grant a right to possession and thereby further strengthen the legal position of the holder, *i.e.* grant him a right that has to be respected by everybody and is especially protected by law. However, these rights *quasi-in rem* only are similar to property rights in some respects and not in others; despite their similarities they are therefore not recognised as rights *in rem*.[83]

a) Rights to Acquire Property

The common feature of rights to acquire property is that the holder is granted a right to acquire either property or a restricted property rights in the future. Examples are the right of appropriation, the right of pre-emption and the notation *in rem*.

The right of appropriation is defined as the right to unilaterally acquire ownership of things, which are ownerless, such as proprietary hunting rights with respect to ownerless animals.

The right of pre-emption confers the right to subrogate to the rights of another party arising from the purchase contract in case immovable property is sold to that third party. The holder of the right of pre-emption accordingly may acquire ownership in place of the owner's contracting partner (§ 1094 in conjunction with § 504).

The notation *in rem* provided for in § 883 ff. serves the absolute protection of an obligatory right to transfer or repeal a property right in immovables. By means of a notation in the land register it gains absolute effect. The notation serves the interest of a purchaser who has already concluded the purchase contract but – due to the principle of abstract tradition – cannot yet be secure that he will later on also acquire ownership. The mere conclusion of a contract does not prevent the

---

[82] Cf. *Ohly*, JZ 2003, 545, 546.

[83] But cf. BVerfG, NJW 1993, 2035 holding that the entitlement of the lessee to possession is within the scope of art. 14 Basic Law, with note by *Depenheuer*, NJW 1993, 2561 ff.

seller from transferring ownership to a third party, even though this would be contrary to his contractual obligation. By means of registration of a notation in favour of the purchaser any disposal of ownership running contrary to such notation will be ineffective with respect to the purchaser (§ 883 subsection 2 sentence 1).

b) Rights of Use and Enjoyment of Property

The group of limited property rights of use and enjoyment contains usufruct, real servitudes in land and restricted personal servitudes.
Usufruct is the most far reaching right to enjoy another's property. It grants the person in whose benefit the usufruct is established an exclusive right to draw the fruits or profits of the thing (§ 1030) and precludes the owner from this opportunity. As the right of usufruct incorporates a strong restriction of the owners exclusive power over his property, the right of usufruct can neither be transferred nor inherited.[84]
Usufruct in movable things, though possible, in practice hardly ever occurs. But a usufruct may be granted with respect to a person's total assets that *inter alia* consist of tangible things.[85] As far as a right of usufruct is granted with respect to consumable things, then the restricted property right is re-interpreted as transfer of ownership in the consumable things. The usufructuary therefore may dispose of the goods, but at the termination of the usufruct is under a duty to compensate the owner of the things for the value, which the things had at the time the usufruct was granted (§ 1067).
A further example of a right to use and enjoy another's property is the real servitude. It grants a restricted right to use another's land: the owner merely devolves certain particular rights of use, such as a right to pass over another's land.
Similarly a restricted personal servitude only restricts particular authorities from the position of ownership and grants them to a particular person. The right of residence or habitation, *i.e.* the right to exclusively use a building or a part of a building (§ 1093), may serve as an example.

c) Security Rights and Power of Sale

The third group of 'other property rights' consists of security rights. In case a secured debt becomes due and yet remains unsettled then the security holder has a

---

[84] *Baur/Stürner*, Sachenrecht[17], § 3 no. 37.
[85] *Baur/Stürner*, Sachenrecht[17], § 49 no. 4.

right to realize the value of the security, usually by means of a power of sale. The Civil Code provides for the security rights of pledge and land charge.
The Civil Code draws a strict distinction between pledge in movable property and pledge in immovable property. Pledge in immovable property can either be a mortgage, a land charge or an annuity charge (cf. § 1113 ff.). All three concepts have the purpose to grant a security in common: the owner grants a pledge in order to secure a debt. In case he is unable or unwilling to discharge the debt if it falls due, the person entitled by the real security has the right to realize the value of the property to satisfy the debts.
In addition to these two security rights expressly provided for by the Civil Code, two further security rights in movables have – despite the *numerus clausus* – been developed *praeter legem*: First, the security interest of the creditor arising from a fiduciary transfer of title and the second, the equitable interest. Both concepts have in common that they divide the right of ownership into a power to use and enjoy property, on the one hand, and a right of security in the property, on the other.[86]
A pledge in movables is the encumbrance of a movable thing that serves the security of an obligation by means of a right to realization. It grants the creditor the right to '*seek satisfaction from the thing*' (§ 1204). The realization may be sought by means of an auction sale of the tangible thing or – in case the thing has a stock-exchange or market price – by means of private sale. However, the right of pledge in movables requires delivery of the thing to the pledgee and accordingly does not allow the above mentioned division between a right to use the property and a security right. As the owner who wants to obtain credit often cannot spare the possibility to use the property, the right of pledge has been increasingly replaced by fiduciary transfer of ownership.[87]
The concept of fiduciary transfer of title is a means to secure an obligation. The party furnishing security transfers ownership to the secured party, subject to the obligatory agreement that the secured party will only dispose of the ownership in case the party furnishing security, *i.e.* the debtor is in default of payment and the obligation thus remains undischarged. The transfer of possession necessary for the transfer of ownership takes place by means of a *constitutum possessorium*. Therefore the debtor remains direct possessor and accordingly retains the right to use and enjoy the property.
Although the secured party formally acquires ownership in the meaning of § 903 this position of conditional ownership must be distinguished from the all-embracing position usually derived from ownership. The underlying concept of conditional ownership is a division between economic ownership, on the one

---

[86] *Baur/Stürner*, Sachenrecht[17], § 49 no. 6.
[87] *Baur/Stürner*, Sachenrecht[17], § 49 no. 4.

hand, and the merely formal (security) ownership, on the other.[88] The ownership of the creditor as the secured party will therefore not unfold full effect before the debtor is either in default of performance or other creditors of the debtor seize the property in the course of enforcement proceedings. The difference between full ownership and mere security ownership is clearly revealed in case of insolvency (*infra § 8*).

At this point a further concept not provided for in the Civil Code, but developed by means of judge made law[89] has to be introduced: the so-called *Anwartschaftsrecht* already mentioned above. An *Anwartschaftsrecht* is an equitable interest. Although not the only, the most important example is the equitable interest of the buyer arising from a sale subject to a reservation-of-title clause: after conclusion of the contract the buyer already obtains possession but – due to the reservation clause – not yet ownership.

The main characteristic of an equitable interest in ownership is that some, but not all requirements of a transfer of a right *in rem* have been met.[90] Therefore the equitable interest is more than a mere expectancy, but still falls short of the full legal position aspired.[91] The minimum requirement of any equitable interest therefore is that the structure of the aspired right and the parties entitled are specified.[92]

The most important application of equitable interest in the present context of law of movable property is the purchase under reservation of title.[93] A reservation of title is characterized by the fact, that ownership is transferred subject to a condition precedent, namely the full discharge of the purchase price. Until this condition is met the seller remains the formal owner of the purchased goods. In fact the purchaser receives possession and thereby acquires the unrestricted right to use and enjoy the property, whereas the seller merely retains the security interest in ownership.

The transferee is granted a legal position similar to the position of ownership, which comprises *inter alia* the right to transfer his position, to grant pledge with respect to the equitable interest obtained or in case of damage to the good claim compensation under tort law. The aggregate of these particular rights arising from

---

88 This was already established by the *Reichsgericht*, see RGZ 45, 80 ff.

89 The Civil Code does contain a provision on reservation of title, which is the most frequent situation that gives rise to an equitable interest. However, the provision of § 449 is contained in the law of obligation and does not provide for the consequences with respect to property law.

90 *Baur/Stürner*, Sachenrecht[17], § 3 no. 44.

91 *Baur/Stürner*, Sachenrecht[17], § 3 no. 46.

92 *Baur/Stürner*, Sachenrecht[17], § 3 no. 46.

93 Equitable interest in immovable property may arise in case of conclusion of a sales contract on real estate prior to the respective entry into the land register or in case a mortgage is agreed upon before the secured debt has arisen.

a sale subject to a reservation-of-title clause are summarized under the term '*Anwartschaftsrecht*' and is hereinafter referred to as 'equitable interest'.
The equitable interest according to the prevailing opinion is a right *in rem*. The Federal Supreme Court has categorized it as a '*wesensgleiches Minus*' (literally a 'similar shortfall of ownership')[94] or an initial stage of ownership[95] respectively. Hence the equitable interest as a general rule is treated subject to the rules of the respective full legal position. In case of a reservation of title clause the corresponding full legal position of course is ownership. In substance the *Anwartschaftsrecht* again is a division between the two main rights provided by ownership, namely the right to use and enjoy property, on the one hand, and the security interest, on the other.[96]

7. Protection of Other Property Rights in Movables

With regard to the protection of restricted property rights the Civil Code again follows the same technique as for the rights themselves: as all 'other property rights' represent a particular aspect of the comprehensive right, *i.e.* ownership, they are accordingly protected by the respective measures that protect the related aspect of ownership. The provisions on restricted property rights therefore refer to the protection of ownership as far as adequate.
As mentioned above the law sets out in detail the means of protection of ownership (§ 985 and § 1004, cf. *supra 5*). The provisions on the restricted property rights then refer to the respective provisions: examples are to be found in § 1065 on usufruct, in § 1227 concerning pledge in movables, in § 1027 and § 1090 subsection 2 for servitudes. The additional protection of property rights provided by the law of unjustified enrichment, tort law as well as public law does not draw any distinction between ownership as the all-embracing right and other restricted property rights.

§ 2. Possession

1. Notion of Possession

The concept of ownership as a definitive order is preceded by the law on possession as a temporary order. Possession thus can be defined as an intentional factual physical control over a thing independent of any legal entitlement. Whereas the concept of ownership concerns the allocation of legal status,

---

[94] BGHZ 28, 16, 21; BGHZ 35, 85, 89.
[95] BGHZ 30, 374, 377.
[96] *Baur/Stürner*, Sachenrecht[17], § 59 no. 33.

possession is characterized by a factual allocation of physical control over movables to persons.[97]

The legal nature of possession has been a matter of long-standing dispute during the 19th century: part of legal doctrine has held possession to be a mere fact, whereas other authors argued in favour of a right.[98] The Civil Code has adopted the second concept. This can be derived both from the rule that possession can be transferred and – even more obvious – from the provision on inheritance of possession (§ 857). A mere factual position could not be transferred by inheritance.

Although the Civil Code acknowledges that possession is a right, it is not considered as a right *in rem* (*dingliches Recht*). Yet, due to its importance for the acquisition and loss of ownership as well as other property rights, it is also regulated in the context of the Third Book under the heading property law (*Sachenrecht*).[99] The main provisions may be found in § 854 ff.

According to § 854 possession of a thing is acquired by obtaining actual power, that is physical control, over the thing.

> **§ 854 BGB [Acquisition of Possession]**
>
> (1) Possession of a thing is acquired by obtaining actual power of control over the thing.
>
> (2) Agreement between the most recent possessor and acquirer is sufficient for the acquisition, if the acquirer is capable of exercising power of control over the thing.

This provision therefore already sets out two of the requirements of possession mentioned above, namely the requirement of factual control[100] and the general[101] restriction to corporeal things in the meaning of § 90 (cf. *infra § 3. 1*). A third – unwritten – requirement is the intention to possess.

Factual control means that the possessor has direct access or rather can directly take hold of the thing. This requires that the person and the thing are in a relationship of proximity of some duration. However, this factual control of the thing need not be exercised directly by the possessor *ad personam*, but instead can

---

97 *Brehm/Berger*, Sachenrecht (2000), no. 2.1.

98 For details see *Brehm/Berger*, Sachenrecht (2000), no. 2.8 ff.

99 The heading of the Third Book 'Property Law' also bears inconsistencies in another respect, because a number of subjects have been provided for, which do not constitute property rights in the meaning of the BGB; for example the usufruct in rights (§§ 1068-1084) or the pledge in a right (§§ 1273-1296), cf. *Brehm/Berger*, Sachenrecht (2000), no. 1.5.

100 An exception from the requirement of physical control is contained in § 857: the heir automatically acquires possession in the event of succession.

101 A further exception from the general rule may be found in § 1029 and § 1090, which recognize the right to possession of servitudes. Although this runs contrary to the concept that there is no possession in rights, this exception is not generalized, cf. *Baur/Stürner*, Sachenrecht[17], § 7 no. 9.

also be held by an intermediary, *i.e.* a direct possessor with the intention to hold possession for the indirect possessor or a possessory servant. As the concept of possession entails a right but not a property right *in rem*, it is further irrelevant whether or not the possessor is entitled to possession: the concept of possession is neutral in relationship to the legal situation. Therefore also al thief is possessor of the stolen goods.
On determining whether a person has physical control over a thing it has to be taken into account, that the act of acquisition of possession (*Besitzerwerb*) requires a more intensive extent of control than the mere continuation of possession (*Besitzerhaltung*).[102] Direct possession once acquired, a person retains this legal position until a cause for termination of possession occurs.[103] An impediment to exercise physical control of a merely temporary nature does not terminate possession (§ 856 subsection 2). For example, a car parked at the parking lot of an airport remains in possession of the possessor who has just commenced his travels during his absence. Similarly, the farmer remains possessor of the plough left on the greenfield overnight. This shows that the intensity of the relation of proximity may vary. Whether or not it is held to be sufficient will be determined according to the so-called common opinion *(Verkehrsauffassung)*.[104]
The second requirement is that the object of possession is a corporeal thing in the meaning of § 90. Due to the narrow definition of thing in the meaning of § 90 and the reference to this concept in § 854, rights cannot be the object of possession.[105] Rights – such as intellectual property rights – do not fall within the scope of *Sachenrecht* and accordingly are not subject to the rules on property law contained in the Third Book.[106] This restriction to corporeal things and the consequence of excluding rights as the object of possession is not contradicted by ‚*Rechtsbesitz*' under § 1029 or § 1090 subsection 2 respectively, as both provisions despite the misleading term[107] do not constitute possession of a right, but rather a right to possess a thing derived from a restricted property right.[108]
The third requirement, the intention to possess, is not expressly mentioned in § 854, but may be derived from a comparison of § 872 and § 854. § 872 provides that a person is called a proprietary possessor (*Eigenbesitzer*), if he possesses the thing as belonging to him, therefore with an *animus rem sibi habendi*. From this

---

[102] *Baur/Stürner*, Sachenrecht[17], § 7 no. 16. The concept of preservation (*Besitzerhaltung*) of possession is criticised by *Brehm/Berger*, Sachenrecht (2000), no. 3.2 (with fn. 1).
[103] *Brehm/Berger*, Sachenrecht (2000), no. 3.2.
[104] BGHZ 101, 186, 187 f.
[105] The concept substituting possession with respect to rights is the related concept of detention.
[106] Cf. *Ohly*, JZ 2003, 545, 546.
[107] Cf. *Brehm/Berger*, Sachenrecht (2000), no. 5.6.
[108] An exception is contained in § 2018 as the possession of estate may also include rights.

provision it can be inferred that the intention with which a person holds physical control in general is of significance. It should be noted, that the intention is directed to possession alone, not to ownership. It is therefore referred to as intention of possessing or *animus possedenti.*
This further requirement has become necessary, because German law has not adopted the Roman law distinction between *possessio* and *detentio*, but instead follows a wide concept of possession. It covers both the situation that a possessor possesses the thing for himself (*Eigenbesitz*) and the situation that a person holds possession for another (*Fremdbesitz).* Therefore the requirement of manifestation of intention to possess is *inter alia* necessary to distinguish between the different types of possession and, in particular, to draw a dividing line between the possessor and the possessory servant according to § 855.
The exact requirements of this manifestation of will necessary to acquire possession are a matter of dispute. Judicature contends itself with a very general *animus possedenti*, which as a rule need not be further specified and will be presumed to exist.[109] The prevailing opinion in legal doctrine demands an indication of the intention to acquire possession (*Besitzbegründungswillen*),[110] though does not pose any strict requirements:[111] the general intention to acquire possession not specified in respect to any particular goods, will suffice. A minority opinion argues that the intention cannot be decisive, but instead it shall suffice that the thing is integrated into the area of organisation (*Organistaionsbereich*) of the acquirer.[112]
A famous and controversial decision of the Federal Supreme Court may serve as an example[113]: A customer lost a banknote in the value of 1000,- German marks between the shelves of a supermarket. Another customer found the banknote, picked it up and handed is over to the employee behind the cashier desk. The Federal Supreme Court has ruled, that neither the customer nor the cashier, but instead the owner of the supermarket obtained direct possession on the basis of its general intention to acquire possession with regard to all things found within the supermarket. This general intention was assumed on the basis that the owner had given directions to his employees to register any goods found in a special notebook and to take them into custody.[114] Similarly, it was decided that an usher

---

[109] RGZ 70, 314, 318.
[110] *Gerhardt*, Mobiliarsachenrecht[4], § 3.2.
[111] BGHZ 101, 186, 187 f.; cf. *Baur/Stürner*, Sachenrecht[17], § 7 no. 15; Staudinger/*Bund* (2000), § 854 no. 18; critical *Gursky*, JZ 1991, 496, 497.
[112] Westermann/*Gursky* § 13 I 2.
[113] BGHZ 101, 186, 187 f.
[114] The decision has been criticised by Staudinger/*Bund* (2000), § 854 no. 18; *Ernst*, JZ 1988, 359 ff., *Gerhardt*, Mobiliarsachenrecht[4] § 4.7. (with fn. 5), Westermann/*Gursky* § 13 I 2 and *Gursky*, JZ 1991, 496, 497, but approved by *Brehm/Berger*, Sachenrecht (2000), no. 3. 10; for further examples see OLG Celle NJW 1992, 2576 and OLG Koblenz NJW-RR 1994, 1351.

who found a diamond ring in the movie theatre did not obtain possession, whereas the owner of the cinema did.[115]

Intention in this context is to be understood as a natural intention and not in the meaning of a legally relevant declaration of will.[116] Therefore a child can also form an intention and acquire possession. As the element of intention is only specified in a very vague way, the requirements of possession draw near to those of 'physical control.'

2. Types of Possession

German law draws a distinction between several different types of possession. It must be emphasized that these different categories are not exclusive, but instead may overlap or be combined. The different types of possession provided for by law, may be distinguished according to

- the intensity of the relationship between the possessor and the asset. German law does distinguish between indirect (*mittelbarer Besitzer*) and direct possessor (*Besitzmittler*);

- the social dependence of the person physically holding the asset from the possessor; a dividing line is drawn between direct possessor (*Besitzmittler*) and possessory servant (*Besitzdiener*).

- the intention of the person holding the asset. A person with *animus rem sibi habendi* is a proprietary possessor (*Eigenbesitzer*) in contrast to a person possessing the asset with the intention to hold it for another (*Fremdbesitzer*).

- the possibility of the possessor to exercise his possession on his own or his dependence on other persons. The former is referred to as sole (or exclusive) possessor, the latter as joint possessor.

a) Direct and Indirect Possession

Direct possession is the prototype of possession and it is defined by § 854: a direct possessor is a person who actually has physical control over the thing. The

[115] According to BGHZ 8, 130 she has obtained physical control in the meaning of §§ 854 and § 965 for her employer and accordingly is merely a possessory servant. Also compare OLG München NJW 1987, 1830.

[116] Staudinger/*Bund* (2000), § 856 no. 15; cf. *Baldus*, JR 2002, 441, 442 f.

opposite of a direct possessor is an indirect possessor as expressly set out by § 868.

> **§ 868 BGB [Indirect Possession]:**
>
> If a person possesses a thing as usufructuary, pledgee, usufructuary lessee, lessee, depositary or in a similar relationship, by virtue of which he is as against another, entitled or obliged for a time to have possession, the other person is also a possessor (indirect possession).

A direct possessor is a person who himself exercises physical control over a thing. An indirect possessor is a person who exercises control by means of legal relationship to the direct possessor.[117] The direct possessor who accounts to an indirect possessor and therefore does not possess the thing with the intention to possess it for himself, but instead respects the indirect possession of another, is referred to as an intermediary in possession (*Besitzmittler*).

The term 'indirect possession' indicates that the possession is not based on physical control but instead on a legal relationship to the direct possessor, *i.e.* the intermediary exercising actual control over the goods.[118] This relationship between indirect and direct possessor is called constructive possession (*Besitzmittlungsverhältnis*) (*infra § 5 4. c*).

Constructive possession may consist of more than one level, therefore the indirect possessor of the second level can possess by means of a legal relationship to the indirect possessor of the first level who again has a legal relationship with the direct possessor exercising direct control.[119]

As far as nothing else is expressly provided for or may be derived from the respective context,[120] direct and indirect possession are both treated similarly as adequate types of possession.[121] The practical relevance of the distinction between direct and indirect possession is, that the concept of indirect possession allows the establishment of indirect possession to substitute actual transfer of possession, a requirement for the transfer of movables under § 930.[122]

---

[117] *Baur/Stürner*, Sachenrecht[17], § 7 no. 4.

[118] *Brehm/Berger*, Sachenrecht (2000), no. 3.12.

[119] For examples see BGH JZ 1964, 130, 132; BGH NJW 1997, 2110, 2111.

[120] Cf. § 935: a thing can only become missing from the direct possessor. Thus § 935 only refers to direct possession.

[121] *Baur/Stürner*, Sachenrecht[17], § 7 no. 50.

[122] *Baur/Stürner*, Sachenrecht[17], § 7 no. 31.

b) Intermediary in Possession and Possessory Servant

Whereas the intermediary possessor mentioned above is a possessor himself, the possessory servant is not considered a possessor, but rather an instrument of the possessor. This concept is set out in § 855.

> **§ 855 BGB [Possessory Servant]**
>
> If a person exercises actual power of control over a thing for another in the latter's household or business, or in a similar relationship by virtue of which he has to comply with the instructions of the other concerning the thing, only such other person is the possessor.

The decisive criterion of a possessory servant is his subordination to the instructions of the possessor, *i.e.* the principal.[123] The underlying legal foundation of the duty to comply with the instructions is irrelevant for the qualification as possessory servant.[124] Apart form the assistant expressly mentioned, all persons who are integrated into another's household, business or other similar form of organisation are possessory servants,[125] as in particular holds true for employees. The difference between an intermediary possessor and a possessory servant is that only the former is considered the holder of a self-standing legal position next to the indirect possessor.[126] By contrast, the possessory servant merely has a factual relationship to the thing. The right of possession is reserved for the principal. Accordingly, a possessory servant does not have any claim arising from possession, neither a right to defend himself against interference of the principal (*Besitzwehr*), nor a right to self-help against his principal (*Besitzkehr*).[127] As the possessory servant is not a possessor himself he is not authorized to transfer possession. In case a possessory servant hands over the thing to a third party without being authorized to do so by the principal, the thing is considered to have become missing in the meaning of § 935 (*infra § 11 8.*).

The concept of possessory servant replaces the *detentio* and is of particular importance for the acquisition of possession (and in consequence ownership) by transfer from or to a *Geheißperson*. Further the assessment of good faith in the context of *bona fide*-acquisition will have to take the respective knowledge of the possessory servant into consideration, not that of the principal (*infra § 11 7.*).

---

[123] BGHZ 16, 259, 264; BGHZ 27, 360, 363; *Baur/Stürner*, Sachenrecht[17], § 7 no. 64.

[124] *Baur/Stürner*, Sachenrecht[17], § 7 no. 67.

[125] *Brehm/Berger*, Sachenrecht (2000), no. 3.32.

[126] *Baur/Stürner*, Sachenrecht[17], § 7 no. 35.

[127] This of course does not preclude his rights against third parties, § 860.

c) Proprietary Possession and Possession in Another's Interest

According to § 872 a person who possesses a thing as belonging to him is a proprietary possessor (*Eigenbesitzer*). The opposite concept of possession in another's interest (*Fremdbesitzer*) is not explicitly defined, but may be derived by an *argumentum e contrario*: A possessor for another person is a person who has physical control over a thing and the intention to hold it on the basis of a restricted right *in rem*, an obligatory right or other legal basis for another person and therefore respects the proprietary possessor's possession.[128]
The distinction between the proprietary possessor and a possessor for another person is based solely on the intention of the respective holder, not on the underlying legal entitlement. Even actual knowledge that another is the authorized owner of a thing is no obstacle for the intention to hold possession as belonging to oneself. Thus a person may transfer possession for another into proprietary possession by changing his mind, *i.e.* decide that from now on the possessor intends to hold the property as his own. However, the change of mind by some means or other has to become apparent for third parties.[129]
The distinction between proprietary possession and possession for another is of some relevance as a number of other provisions specify the requirement of possession by the term of proprietary possession (and thereby tacitly refer to § 872). This further requirement for example may be found in § 937 on acquisitive prescription, the acquisition of fruits and profits of the *bona fide* possessor (§ 988) and in particular in the provision on presumption of ownership in favour of the possessor (§ 1006). But of course, also the transfer of possession under § 929 ff. as a general rule requires transfer of proprietary possession.

d) Exclusive Possession and Joint-Possession

The main characteristic of this further distinction is the possibility to exercise physical control. A sole possessor exercises exclusive physical control, *i.e.* without any restrictions of his position as possessor by others. A particular type of sole possession is partial possession in the meaning of § 865. Here the partial possessor has exclusive control over a part of a thing. For instance a lessee has exclusive control of his part of the house, *i.e.* the apartment. Partial possession is adequate possession and has all functions of possession.[130]
The opposite of sole possession is joint possession, which is further divided into simple joint possession (*schlichter Mitbesitz*) and joint possession (*gesamthänderischen Mitbesitz*). In case of simple joint possession each of the

---

[128] *Baur/Stürner*, Sachenrecht[17], § 7 no. 89.
[129] *Brehm/Berger*, Sachenrecht (2000), no. 3.26
[130] *Baur/Stürner*, Sachenrecht[17], § 7 no. 76.

joint possessors can exercise physical control over the goods but must be considerate of the other joint possessors. The situation that several persons each have a key to a treasure chest and therefore can independently gain access to it may serve as an example for simple joint possession.[131]
By contrast the co-possessors of a joint possession can only exercise their possession by acting together. This can be demonstrated by the above mentioned example of the treasure chest. In case it has two different locks and each of the co-possessors has the key to one of the locks, then both have to join together in order to gain access to the contents of the treasure box. For factual reasons the physical control therefore can only be exercised in co-operation.[132]
With regard to third parties both simple joint possession and joint possession are adequate possession. Restrictions however exist with respect to the internal relationship between the joint or co-possessors as no protection of possession is afforded vis-à-vis each other (Cf. § 866).

3. The Different Functions of Possession

The term functions of possession (*Funktionen des Besitzes*) is frequently used as an umbrella term for the protective function of possession, the function of possession as a means to transfer ownership and make such transfer public and the function to maintain possession. These concepts all indicate that the concept of possession – although in itself not recognized as a right *in rem* – is a legal position protected by law, which is of importance in other contexts, in particular with respect to acquisition and loss of property rights in movables. The concept of possession therefore is a legal technique of simplification, as all other concepts merely have to include the term 'possession' and thereby refer to § 854 ff.
Because of these function the interest of the possessor to maintain possession is recognized and protected. The protection afforded to possession at the same time affords protection to all other legal concepts that *inter alia* contain a right to possession, even though they may be of a merely obligatory nature.

a) Protection of Possession

As possession is a requirement for different legal consequences, it is afforded particular protection in three respects (*Schutzfunktion*). § 859 grants the possessor a right of self-help against unlawful interference, § 861 a claim against unlawful deprivation of possession and § 862 a claim for abatement of nuisance and cessation of interference. By means of these protective measures the possessor is

---

[131] Cf. BGH NJW 1979, 714, 715; BGH NJW 1993, 935, 936.
[132] *Brehm/Berger*, Sachenrecht (2000), no. 3.28.

granted similar strength of protection against any third party as against the owner.[133]

b) Transfer and Publicity

Transfer of ownership of a movable requires a real agreement and delivery (cf. § 929). Delivery of course is nothing else than transfer of possession.
Both in the common interest of all persons participating in legal transactions and as a prerequisite for the respect of absolute rights by all other members of society, the existence, transfer and loss of absolute rights in property have to be made public. As far as movable property is concerned this rationale of publicity is realized by the concept of possession. The transfer of possession in movables therefore – according to the concept of the legislator – is a means of making the change of allocation of rights *in rem* apparent for third parties and thus is the mechanism to adhere to the principle of publicity (*Publizitätsfunktion*).
The concept that ownership and possession are supposed to correspond leads to two important consequences:
First, § 1006 in favour of the possessor of a movable thing presumes that he is the owner of the thing.[134] Although this presumption may be rebutted, it leads to a shift of the burden of proof and therefore is of great importance in the context of litigation. The presumption of ownership further provides the basis for the legitimate expectation of an acquirer that the possessor is authorized to dispose of the property.
Second, the possession of a thing regularly is a prerequisite of a valid transfer of title in movables, both by an authorized as by an unauthorized person. Possession accordingly has a transfer function.
In order to facilitate and make secure legal transactions and to relieve the individual from the burden to scrutinize the authority of the transferor in each legal transaction, the law provides for the possibility to acquire property from an unauthorized person. The minimum requirement for this however is that the acquirer is in good faith in respect to the authority of the transferor. This good faith is based on the legitimizing appearance of possession. This legitimizing appearance includes the power to transfer possession or to instruct another to transfer possession respectively (cf. *infra § 5 4. c*).

---

[133] As to the specific protective measures cf. *infra 5.*
[134] BGH FamRZ 1970, 586 with note *Hadding*, JuS 1972, 183 f.; OLG Hamburg MDR 1974, 754; BGH NJW-RR 1989, 651.

c) Preservation of Possession

A person who possesses property may have a legitimate interest in retaining property whether or not he is entitled to possession by a right *in rem* or merely by an obligatory right. The law recognizes this interest in various contexts and protects the possessor, who has a right to possession, against the consequences of contrary dispositions of the owner. It preserves possession (*Erhaltungsfunktion*). Evidence of this preservative function can be found in the following situations:
In case the owner sells a movable asset rented to the possessor, the possessor is protected against the loss of possession. As the possessor derives his entitlement to posses from a lease contract concluded between him and the owner, the owner may transfer ownership, but thereby cannot deprive him of his right to possession. In case the new owner claims delivery the lessee can invoke the defence of § 986 subsection 2 and retain possession.
In case the creditors of the owner seek enforcement against the owner and threaten to seize the asset from the possessor, the possessor has a right to redeem the debt. He can discharge the debt rendering an opposing will of both creditor and debtor irrelevant and can as a consequence retain possession (§ 268 subsection 1 sentence 2). The creditor in turn is obliged to assign the right to him.
A further emanation of the function of preservation is the concept of acquisitive prescription. By virtue of a long-lasting subsistence, possession can strengthen to the right of ownership. As far as movable property is concerned the requirements for prescriptive acquisition according to § 937 ff. are ten years of quiet *bona fide* possession as a proprietary possessor (cf. *infra § 12 1.*).

4. Acquisition of Possession

a) Title for Acquisition of Possession

The right to hold or acquire possession from the owner may either arise from a right *in rem* or be of an obligatory nature. As mentioned above the Civil Code contains a *numerus clausus* of rights *in rem*. As far as movable property is concerned there are only three property rights which give the title-holder a right to possession: the all-embracing right of ownership and the two acknowledged restricted rights *in rem*, namely usufruct and pledge. Examples for obligatory rights which comprise a right to possession are tenancy or lease.
Attention should be drawn to an important difference: a person, who holds a right *in rem* entitling him to possession may claim transfer of possession from any other person. By contrast the protection against the respective contractual partner arising from obligatory relationships follows the rules of the law of obligations. Accordingly, a lessee can only claim transfer of property from the lessor, but not from another person who has obtained the asset by a deliberate act of the owner.

Yet, once the person entitled by an obligatory right has obtained possession of the asset, the obligatory right gains strength: The rules on protection of possession according to § 859 ff. are applicable (*supra 3. a*). Similarly, the right of defence against a claim for surrender by the owner is granted to the possessor, independent of whether the basis of this entitlement to possess arises from a right *in rem* or is of an obligatory nature. An obligatory right strengthened by possession accordingly is often referred to as a right *quasi-in rem.*
The specific protection therefore is merely interrelated by the legal position of possession and is independent both of the underlying title and the duration of the entitlement. Whether or not the underlying obligation is valid or void, gratuitous of for consideration is equally irrelevant for the protection afforded.
It follows from the fact that the protection afforded is linked to possession that an obligatory claim for delivery or subsequent transfer of possession does not fall within the scope of the protection. Therefore a principal, who has instructed his agent to acquire possession, but who now refuses to transfer possession to the principal, will have to rely on the obligatory remedies afforded by the underlying mandate relationship. He has no right *in rem* against the agent. Of course the principal could prevent this result by prior agreement to an anticipated *constitutum possessorium* (though according to the judicature the agent will even then not be bound by the real agreement, cf. *infra § 5 3.*).

b) Acquisition of Physical Control

The basic norm for the acquisition of possession is § 854: ‚*possession is acquired by obtaining actual power of control over the thing*'. This provision comprises both derivative and original acquisition of possession. Acquisition of possession is derivative if the possessor by transfer derives his position from the former possessor. Original acquisition means that the possessor has gained actual power over the thing without regard to the intention of the former possessor, because the latter either does not consent or because the thing had become derelict. Both ways of acquisition as a rule lead to adequate positions, namely possession in the meaning of § 854.
The distinction between derivative and original acquisition is of relevance as far as acquisition of possession is a requirement of the transfer of ownership of movables according to § 929 ff. These rules naturally demand transfer and thus derivative acquisition of possession. The same holds true for *bona fide*-acquisition: § 935 excludes *bona fide*-acquisition with respect to such things which 'have become missing' and consequently refers to the manner in which the owner has lost possession. If he has handed over the thing to another deliberately – who has in consequence obtained derivative possession – *bona fide*-acquisition

is approved; if otherwise, the thing is considered to have become missing and *bona fide*-acquisition is excluded[135] (cf. *infra § 11 8.*).
Leaving aside specific rules[136] transfer of derivative possession requires a real agreement and transfer of physical control. The real agreement consists of two elements. First, the former possessor's declaration of will to hand over possession and second, the declaration of will of the acquirer to obtain possession. It is important to distinguish this real agreement on the transfer of possession from the real agreement on the transfer of ownership, even though both more often than not will coincide.[137]
The real agreement on transfer of possession is a legal act and therefore – as all real agreements concerning property rights – subject to the rules of the General Part of the Civil Code (First Book).[138] In consequence the real agreement for example may be avoided in case of a defective declaration of will.[139]
By contrast the manifestation of intention to obtain property by original acquisition is considered a merely factual act and therefore is not subject to the rules on legal transactions: thus also a child lacking legal capacity can obtain possession by original acquisition.[140]
As mentioned above, the general rule for obtaining physical control over a thing is the actual transfer of possession. But already § 854 subsection 2 contains a far-reaching exception. In addition further means to substitute actual transfer of possession are acknowledged.
According to § 854 subsection 2 actual transfer of physical control can be replaced by an agreement between the most recent possessor and the acquirer, if the acquirer subsequently is capable of exercising power of control over the thing. Actual transfer of possession (*traditio vera*) therefore can be substituted by an agreement on the transfer of possession (*traditio ficta*). The comparison with the general rule clearly shows that this alternative contains an alleviation with respect to the requirement of proximity between person and thing. A common textbook example is a stack of wood in the forest: the acquisition of property does not demand that former possessor and acquirer actually go to the wood and the acquirer takes over physical control. Instead the transfer may also take place in –

---

135 If for example the agreement on transfer of possession was void due to a lack of capacity of the former possessor, then the thing is held to have become missing in the meaning of § 935: the transferee may obtain possession but not (*bona fide*) ownership.
136 Such as merger or inheritance law.
137 BGH, NJW 1979, 714.
138 *Baur/Stürner*, Sachenrecht[17], § 7 no. 22; *Brehm/Berger*, Sachenrecht (2000), no. 3.8. and no. 27.13. However, exceptions may be considered as far as this is necessary with respect to the abstract nature, *Rinne* in: MünchKomm BGB[4] VI, Introduction, no. 8.
139 This though does not result in the thing having become missing in the meaning of § 935, *Baur/Stürner*, Sachenrecht[17], § 7 no. 23.
140 Cf. *Brehm/Berger*, Sachenrecht (2000), no. 3.10.

for instance – an office, if (i) the transferor is possessor of the stack of wood and (ii) the acquirer obtains the possibility to exercise exclusive physical control over the stack of wood.

Likewise it may be sufficient to hand over a key to transfer physical control over the things that are secured by the respective lock. For example the things that are contained in a locked treasure chest are in the possession of the person who has the key (and knows where the treasure chest is).[141] By contrast, a merely symbolic transfer which does not afford the acquirer physical control in general is not recognized. Accordingly the attachment of a sign[142] or a short test drive of the employee of the acquirer are insufficient, if the thing subsequently remains in the organisational area of the (former) possessor.[143] Symbolic transfer will only suffice as far as provided by special provisions.[144]

Apart from the replacement of a *traditio vera* by a *traditio ficta*, the handing over of physical control may in addition be substituted by one of the following transfer modes:

§ 868 provides that possession can also be transferred by the agreement on a relationship of constructive possession (*constitutum possessorium*). This is an agreement between the transferor as the (in-)direct possessor and the transferee, that the transferor will from now on exercise possession for the transferee. The transferor becomes a possessor for another, the transferee obtains indirect proprietary possession.

For the agreement on a valid *constitutum possessorium* three criteria must be met: (i) the transferor must hold possession in the interest of another, (ii) the relationship of constructive possession must be limited in time and (iii) the constructive possession must be based on an underlying legal justification

The first precondition of a *constitutum possessorium* is that the direct possessor obtains possession and has the intention to possess for the indirect possessor (for instance as the lessee or usufructuary) and not as an owner (*Fremdbesitzwillen*).[145] The direct possessor must therefore derive his right of possession from the legal position of the indirect possessor.[146]

The second condition is that the relationship of constructive possession must be restricted to a limited period of time. This may already be derived from a literal

---

[141] BGH DB 1973, 913; BGH NJW 1979, 713; OLG Düsseldorf NJW-RR 1996, 839, 841.

[142] OLG Frankfurt BB 1976, 573.

[143] OLG München NJW 1970, 667.

[144] For instance transfer of possession (and title) by transfer of bearer's instruments.

[145] Cf. RGZ 135, 75, 78.

[146] Thus the seller who has already sold the good but not yet handed it over to the purchaser is not an intermediary possessor for the purchaser; cf. *Baur/Stürner*, Sachenrecht[17], § 7 no. 37.

interpretation of § 868.[147] It is also a consequence of the concept of indirect possession: it necessarily contains a claim for delivery. The indirect possessor therefore must have a claim for recovery against the direct possessor,[148] which of course may be subject to conditions precedent or subsequent such as lapse of time.[149]

The list of relationships a constructive possession may be based on contained in § 868 has lead to the development of a further requirement, namely that the underlying relationship must be specified, *i.e.* set out the rights and duties of the parties to the agreement (*konkretes Besitzmittlungsverhältnis*).[150]

In addition to the legal relationships enlisted in § 868, all similar relationships provide a sufficient basis, provided they rely on a contract (*e.g.* sale under reservation of title), statute (*e.g.* parental care and custody) or an act of state (administration of estate in bankruptcy).[151] By contrast it would not suffice to agree on a formal relationship of constructive possession, that is the mere agreement that the transferor from now on intends to possess for the transferee without specification of a legal basis from which this duty may arise.[152] The rationale of this restriction, however, is not to be found in the law on possession itself, but actually is a consequence of the role of possession for the transfer of title. The rules on transfer of ownership hold a relationship of constructive possession to be a sufficient substitute for actual transfer (§ 930). Therefore the acceptance of a formal relationship of constructive possession would lead to the result, that the parties could dispose of the transfer requirement.[153] For example A and B could agree that A will henceforth hold the property for B, even though an underlying legal justification for this transfer (such as lease, fiduciary transfer of title) is lacking. In order to prevent this result, a specified underlying relationship of constructive possession is demanded.

Despite this intention the validity of this underlying agreement according to the prevailing opinion is not a condition for the constructive possession to meet the requirements. The minimum requirement is that the intermediary on the basis of the (invalid) agreement respects the proprietary possession of the direct possessor and exercises control with the intention to hold it for his contracting partner.[154]

---

[147] BGHZ 85, 263, 265; the judicature in BGHZ 73, 253, 257 has also recognized marriage to be a valid relationship of indirect possession, although it of course is not concluded for a limited period of time, cf. *Brehm/Berger*, Sachenrecht (2000), no. 3.14.

[148] *Brehm/Berger*, Sachenrecht (2000), no. 3.14.

[149] BGHZ 85, 263, 265.

[150] Cf. BGHZ 73, 253, 257.

[151] Cf. *Baur/Stürner*, Sachenrecht[17], § 7 no. 48.

[152] Of other opinion *Wacke*, ZEuP 2000, 254, 260.

[153] *Brehm/Berger*, Sachenrecht (2000), no. 3.15.

[154] BGH NJW 1955, 499; BGH WM 1985, 1433; BGHZ 85, 263, 265 against the previous judicature: RGZ 86, 265 and RGZ 98, 133. Cf. *Wieling*, AcP 184 (1984), 439, 440 ff.

The underlying relationship can even be agreed upon before the transferor (and future direct possessor for another) has himself obtained possession. This construction is called an anticipated *constitutum possessorium* (*antezipierten Besitzkonstituts*). The moment the transferor obtains possession and has formed the intention to hold it for the transferee the latter acquires indirect possession. The same result can be achieved, if the transferee grants the transferor authority to enter into a legal transaction in the name of the transferee as the principal and himself in his own name as the transferor (§ 181) and thereby establishes a relationship of constructive possession.[155]

A further substitute for actual transfer is the assignment of the claim for recovery of possession to the acquirer. This mode of transfer is of particular importance, if the thing to be transferred is in the hands of a third party (cf. § 931 and *infra § 5 4. c*). The assignment of the claim follows the rules of § 398 and accordingly does not require any notification of the direct possessor. However, the application of § 398 also leads to the result that the assignment of the claim may be barred by an agreement between direct and indirect possessor. In this case the assignment is invalid (§ 399 2nd case) and in consequence the transfer of indirect possession according to § 870 fails.[156]

An exception from the rule, that transfer of possession requires at least (substitute) transfer of physical control may be found in § 857. In the event of succession the possession of the deceased is automatically transferred to the heirs. This rule is necessary, because German law does not adopt the concept of a *hereditas iacens*. If the heir would not automatically acquire possession by a *traditio ficta*, then the estate would be in no one's possession. As this would lead to the consequence that nobody could invoke the protective measures, it is deemed that the heirs immediately acquire possession, whether or not they know that the deceased has died or what they have inherited and even where these assets are. Things taken from the estate without the consent of the heirs, therefore are held to be missing in the meaning of § 935.[157] The rule of § 857 is extended beyond its scope of literal interpretation and also applied to other cases of universal succession, such as the merger of two companies.[158]

---

155 Cf. BGH NJW 1964, 398.

156 Accordingly this leads to a lack of substitute transfer mode for the transfer of ownership under § 931. Neither are the requirements of a transfer of ownership under § 934 met, because possession is not subject to *bona fide*-acquisition.

157 *Baur/Stürner*, Sachenrecht[17], § 8 no. 2.

158 *Baur/Stürner*, Sachenrecht[17], § 8 no. 4; *Brehm/Berger*, Sachenrecht (2000), no. 3.31.

c) Loss of Possession

Loss of possession occurs if the holder gives up possession or if he looses possession in another way, whether deliberate or involuntarily. The distinction between voluntary and involuntary loss of (in-)direct possession is of particular importance in the context of *bona fide*-acquisition: a thing that has been stolen or has become missing cannot be acquired in good faith (cf. § 932 ff. and *infra § 12 8.*).

Loss of possession of the direct possessor may be the result of loss or theft. The indirect possessor in addition will loose possession in case the intermediary gives up or looses possession. Loss of possession may further occur, if a possessor for another changes his mind and decides to henceforth possess as a proprietary possessor or in case the possessory servant deprives the possessor of his possession by unlawful interference. Whereas a merely temporary impediment to exercise control does not terminate possession (§ 856 subsection 2).

5. Protection of Possession

Rules on protection of possession may be found in § 858 ff. and are directed against unlawful interference, that is interference with quiet enjoyment of possession or deprivation of possession.

The protected object is *direct* possession. Therefore the direct possessor can invoke protective measures against the indirect possessor, whereas the indirect possessor is not protected and cannot rely on protective measures to deprive the direct possessor of his position. He will have to (apply to the court and) rely on the claim arising from the relationship of constructive possession.[159]

With respect to third parties both a proprietary possessor or a possessor for another can invoke the protective measures. In case the direct possessor's possession is interfered with, also the indirect possessor can take the measures provided for. By virtue of § 860 a similar right is granted to the possessory servant, who may invoke the rights in place of the possessor. As far as the protective measures in case of unlawful interference are concerned, it has to be distinguished between emergency rights and applications to the court.

The general rule is, that every deprivation of possession or interference with quiet possession, which takes place without the consent of the possessor, is unlawful and constitutes unlawful interference in the meaning of § 858, unless permitted by statute (cf. *infra*). The dividing line between deprivation of possession and interference with quiet possession is not always clear. Both forms of unlawful interference have in common that the possession of the direct possessor is by some means disturbed by a third party. As the legal consequences of both forms

---

[159] *Baur/Stürner*, Sachenrecht[17], § 9 no. 24.

of interference are similar, the distinction is of no great relevance, apart from the different time limits for protective measures (cf. § 859 subsection 2 and § 861 subsection 2).
The act will not be unlawful if it is permitted by statute. Such rights to interfere with another's possession may *inter alia* be based on performance of an official duty such as the court officer who seizes property in the course of enforcement action (§ 808 subsection 1 ZPO) or the provisions of §§ 227, 229, 859 and § 904 (emergency rights and self-help).
A person who obtains possession by unlawful interference is possessor, but a *mala fide* possessor in the meaning of § 858 subsection 2. This defect continues if possession is transferred either by inheritance or to another who has knowledge of the defect: the new possessor in this case again only obtains defective possession, § 858 subsection 2 sentence 2. The defect, however, is restricted to the relationship between the former possessor unlawfully dispossessed and the new possessor, whereas in respect of third parties the new possessor has all rights arising from possession. Even the thief may therefore protect his possession against third parties by invoking § 859 ff.

a) Emergency Rights

Emergency rights are provided for in § 859 and § 860: in case of impending interference with possession § 859 subsection 1 grants the possessor the right to use force and defend himself against this interference. This right is called defence of possession (*Besitzwehr*) and is a specific emanation of self-defence (§ 227).[160] The permission lasts as long as interference is impending or continuing.
In case of dispossession of movable property, the possessor has the right to retake it by force from a violator caught red-handed (§ 859 subsection 2/3). This so-called right of return of possession (*Besitzkehr*) is a specific manifestation of self-help.[161] It is permissible even if the act of dispossession has already taken place and the violator has successfully obtained possession. The (former) possessor may take necessary measures to recover possession.[162] But it has to take place promptly, *i.e.* as soon as possible. Both rights are similarly granted to the possessory servant (§ 860) and to the indirect possessor (§ 869).

b) Remedies

In case the emergency rights have expired or the (former) possessor does not want to make use of these rights, he can apply to the courts and claim abatement of

[160] *Baur/Stürner*, Sachenrecht[17], § 9 no. 11.
[161] *Baur/Stürner*, Sachenrecht[17], § 9 no. 11.
[162] See BayObLG NJW 1965, 163; OLG Koblenz MDR 1978, 141.

nuisance, cessation of interference and resumption of possession against the violator. Dependant on whether he relies on the fact of his former possession or invokes a superior right to possession, it is distinguished between possessory protection (*possessorischer Rechtsschutz*) and competitive protection of possession (*petitorischer Rechtsschutz*).
Possessory protection is established by a claim for recovery of possession (§ 861) and cessation of disturbance (§ 862). Both remedies are granted irrespective of the legal entitlement to possess, that is whether or not the applicant has a better title to possess than the violater. The mere fact of former possession will suffice.
These protective measures have to be enforced by legal process. The aim of these protective measures is the preservation of the former *status quo*. The main feature of these proceedings therefore is that the violator cannot bring forward any objections. He cannot justify his act by asserting that he is entitled to possession. Even in case he was, he is not allowed to enforce his right by means of unlawful interference. Thus even the owner of the property would be defeated, his claim of superior entitlement rendered irrelevant by the exclusion of objections (§ 863).[163]
Both the claim on account of deprivation of possession (§ 861) and the claim on account of interference with possession (§ 862) can be enforced by legal action and in case of urgency be secured by an injunction. Both claims are extinguished upon the lapse of the year following unlawful interference.
The so-called competitive protection (*petitorischer Rechtsschutz*) is provided for by § 1007. The former possessor of movable goods is granted the right to demand the return of the thing from the recent possessor, if the latter was not in good faith when obtaining possession, or if the thing has become missing from the former possessor. § 1007 is an extension of the presumption of ownership in § 1006 and protects the person who has the superior entitlement to possession. By contrast to the possessory protection mentioned above, the aim of this measure is not merely to return to the *status quo*, but instead to conclusively resolve the conflict between the former and the recent possessor: the defendant may bring forward all objections against the claim for resumption of possession.
This competitive protection is of relevance in cases where the former possessor has a superior entitlement to possession, but can neither rely on any other substantive right (such as ownership, other property rights or a claim arising from unlawful interference).[164] This in particular concerns the lessee or leaseholder,

[163] OLG Düsseldorf MDR 1971, 1011; OLG Köln MDR 1995, 1215. However, the defendant can introduce his defence by way of counterclaim and in case both claims are rdue for decision the defendant may succeed with his reliance on a better entitlement to possession, cf. BGH NJW 1979, 1358; *Lehmann-Richter*, NJW 2003, 1717, 1718.
[164] *Baur/Stürner*, Sachenrecht[17], § 9 no. 27.

who wants to reclaim possession from a third party or defend himself against unlawful interference by such third party.[165]
In addition to these specific remedies granted by the law of possession, the possessor can in case of negligent or wilful interference claim damages arising from tort law provisions under § 823 subsection 1.[166] As far as his (obligatory) right to possession is (or has been) strengthened by actual possession, this possession constitutes ‚*another right*' in the meaning of § 823.[167] The damage in this case consists of the loss of profits or the loss of value the property has suffered as a result of the dispossession of other interference with the property.[168] Similarly, a claim *ex* unjustified enrichment may arise, either a *condictio indebiti*[169] or a *condictio possessionis*[170] under § 812.

§ 3. Ownership in Movables

1. Scope of Application

The Civil Code draws a strict distinction between the rules on the acquisition of property rights in corporeal goods or land and the acquisition of rights. The acquisition of rights is solely provided for by the law of obligations and therefore is excluded from the scope of application of property law. Within property law there is a further fundamental distinction, namely between movable property and immovables.
In order to discuss the transfer of title in movables it is necessary to specify the scope of application of the rules on acquisition of movable property. To this end we therefore have to first discuss the concept of a 'thing' in the meaning of § 90 and subsequently differentiate between movable and immovable property.

a) The Concept of a 'Thing'

The Civil Code has adopted a very narrow concept of ‚thing' (*Sachen*).[171] According to § 90 a thing in the meaning of this provision is a corporeal object, which is perceptible and susceptible of human control. By virtue of this definition a wide range of assets is excluded, in particular rights such as intellectual property

---

[165] Cf. *Baur/Stürner*, Sachenrecht[17], § 9 no. 16.
[166] *Baur/Stürner*, Sachenrecht[17], § 9 no. 31 ff.
[167] BGHZ 73, 355, 362; BGHZ 114, 305.
[168] BGH NJW 1979, 2035.
[169] RGZ 129, 307, 311.
[170] BGH NJW 1979, 2034.
[171] *Rinne* in: MünchKomm BGB[4] VI, Introduction, no. 3.

rights and receivables.[172] But also electricity[173] and computer programmes[174] are excluded as they do not qualify as tangible assets. Only the data carrier itself, on which the latter are stored, will be a thing in the meaning of § 90.[175]
Further exclusions from the definition of a corporeal object concern human beings. Human beings are the holders of rights not their objects. This exclusion of human beings as well as the body of a deceased person is a consequence of the right to protection of one's personality and of the individual sphere of privacy.
However, it is a matter of dispute inhowfar this exclusion also applies to separated parts of the human body (such as vital body parts for an organ transplantation[176] or semen[177]) and whether these can be the object of real agreements. According to the judicature of the Federal Supreme Court body parts only share the legal category of human beings as far and as long as they are separated with the intention to later reintegrate them into (another) human body.[178] By contrast a permanent separation leads to their qualification as a corporeal thing in the meaning of § 90.
In 1990 a new § 90a was introduced into the Civil Code by statutory act, stating explicitly that animals are not things.[179] However, § 90 sentence 2 provides, that the provisions on corporeal things shall be applied to animals as far as nothing else is explicitly provided for. Such particular provisions have at the same time been adopted, *e.g.* in § 251 subsection 2 with respect to damages and in particular for expenses incurred for the treatment of an injured animal. As far as transfer of title is concerned, there are, however, no particular rules for animals.

b) Movables

The Civil Code refers to movable property (*e.g.* in § 929, § 937, § 946) as the opposite of real property, *i.e.* immovables, but does not define the term of movable property. The definition therefore has to be inferred from the definition of immovable property.

---

172 *Baur/Stürner*, Sachenrecht[17], § 3 no. 2.
173 Staudinger/*Stieper* (2004), § 90 no. 10.
174 Staudinger/*Stieper* (2004), § 90 no. 13.
175 BGHZ 102, 135, 144; *Baur/Stürner*, Sachenrecht[17], § 3 no. 2, 11; *Brehm/Berger*, Sachenrecht (2000), no. 1.50.
176 The transplantation of human organs is now provided for by a separate statute, Transplantation Act of November 5th, 1997, BGBl I, 2631.
177 BGHZ 124, 52, 54, with critical note *Taupitz*, NJW 1995, 745 ff.
178 See the criticism of *Taupitz*, NJW 1995, 745; see further Staudinger/*Stieper* (2004), § 90 no. 22.
179 The provision has been subject of harsh criticism and is said to be meaningless, see for instance *Baur/Stürner*, Sachenrecht[17], § 3 no. 4 and *Brehm/Berger*, Sachenrecht (2000), no. 1.54.

A piece of real estate is a defined part of the earth's surface as it is registered in the land register.[180] By contrast all distinct tangible things that are susceptible of human control are corporeal corporeal objects, unless they qualify either as real estate or – by exception – as an essential constituent part of real estate. Essential component parts in the meaning of §§ 93, 94 have lost their ability to be the object of separate property rights and share the legal status of the respective piece of land.

Essential component parts (*wesentlicher Bestandteil*) of a thing according to § 93 are defined as such parts, which cannot be separated without either of the parts thereby being destroyed or substantially altered in its character. Examples for essential component parts of real estate are buildings or particular fixtures (*e.g.* heating,[181] bathtubs,[182] gas or electric kitchen stoves,[183] an emergency back-up generator[184]). Likewise, natural products which have not yet been harvested will qualify as essential component parts (*e.g.* fruit hanging on the tree, a tree not yet lumbered, the crop on the field) and therefore share the legal status of the principal thing (the fruit tree, the tree, the soil of the field). Thus they themselves are not subject to the rules on movables.

The opposite of an essential component part may be found in the concept of an independent part or accessory, *i.e.* a movable which without being an essential component part of the principal thing is attached to another thing

Whether a thing is considered to be an independent part or a component part of another thing – whether movable or immovable – is decided according to common opinion (*Verkehrsauffassung*).[185] On deciding, whether a thing is an essential component part and therefore unable to retain a separate legal status or by contrast an independent (component) part, the judicature also takes economic reasoning into consideration. Thus for instance the standard engine of a car already built into a passenger car, was not considered an essential component part, but an independent accessory.[186] Likewise, the tires of a passenger car were held to be independent parts.[187] However, these rulings have been criticized by legal doctrine as they do not actually rely on the definition contained in § 90 ff., but instead focus on the economic results.

Similarly accessories in the meaning of § 97 constitute independent parts. Accessories as a general rule share the legal status of the principal thing. In case

---

[180] *Baur/Stürner*, Sachenrecht[17], § 3 no. 5.
[181] BGH NJW-RR 1990, 158.
[182] OLG Braunschweig, Ns. RPflg 1955, 193.
[183] BGH NJW 1953, 1180.
[184] BGH NJW 1987, 3187.
[185] *Brehm/Berger*, Sachenrecht (2000), no. 1.53.
[186] BGHZ 61, 80, 81; in agreement *Baur/Stürner*, Sachenrecht[17], § 3 no. 8; but criticised by *Brehm/Berger*, Sachenrecht (2000), no. 55.
[187] BayObLG, NVwZ 86, 511.

the principal thing is transferred, it is presumed that the transfer also includes the accessories and renders a separate transfer of the accessories superfluous. Therefore the requirements of transfer of title under §§ 929 ff. need not be met with respect to the accessories. As the intention of the legislator is that accessories shall share the legal status of the principal thing, they may not be seized separately in the course of enforcement (cf. § 865 subsection 2 ZPO). Yet, the owner can transfer accessories separately according to the general rules on transfer of movables.[188]

An exception from the general rule that accessories follow the legal status of the principal thing is contained in § 95: things do not become constituent parts of a piece of land if they are attached to the soil for a merely temporary purpose. A garage put up only for the duration of the lease may serve as an example.[189] These objects are called '*Scheinbestandteile*' and can be subject to separate legal transactions. The rules on transfer of title in movables apply accordingly.[190]

As far as the Civil Code regulates whether a thing is movable of immovable and whether it is an independent part or a essential component part of another thing, these rules are of mandatory nature and therefore cannot be altered by agreement of the parties. Such an agreement may – if at all – at most have an obligatory effect.

2. Specific Provisions on Co-Ownership

a) Simple Joint Ownership (by Shares)

In general the rules on transfer of title in movables do also apply both to the transfer of a share in simple joint ownership and to the transfer of the entire object of joint ownership.

Simple joint ownership may for instance arise in case of *commixtio* or *confusio* of distinct tangible things according to the rules of §§ 947, 948 (cf. *infra § 10*). As a result each co-owner is entitled to a fraction of undivided shares. The substance of this fraction of undivided shares, however, in fact is a share in the value or a right to use the common property.

Each respective fraction is treated as a separate object of property law and can be transferred independently of the other fractions. Thus the individual co-owner is holder of a separate property right of which he can dispose independently, *i.e.* without the consent of the other co-owners.

---

188 For example BGH ZIP 1994, 305.

189 BGHZ 8, 1, 6; BGH NJW 1985, 789.

190 BGHZ 23, 57, 59; BGH NJW 1987, 774.

The separate shares can be transferred according to the general rules on transfer of title in movables. The acquirer becomes the successor to the specific shares as the transferor held them. However, § 751 sentence 1 applies and contains an important alteration. In case the participants have permanently or for a specific time excluded the right to demand dissolution of co-ownership or have fixed a period for notice, this agreement is valid both in favour and against a successor in title. The same holds true for agreements on use and administration of the common property, which remain valid. The rules on *bona fide*-acquisition of unencumbered property rights insofar are precluded.
In case the common property as such is supposed to be transferred, the authority for this transaction lies with the joint co-owners. If they transfer all their shares to a single third party, the separate shares dissolve and the third party acquires undivided property.

b) Joint Ownership

Joint ownership or so-called partnership property is a separate asset and is held by the joint co-owners conjointly. They can therefore only together dispose of the partnership property. The individual cannot dispose of his undivided interest, § 719 subsection 1.
Examples of such partnership property would be the decedent's estate in case of a plurality of heirs (§ 2032 ff.), community property of spouses (§ 1415 ff.) or the company assets of a partnership (§ 718). Leaving this restriction of authority to dispose aside, the transfer of joint ownership follows the general rules on transfer in movables.

Part II: Derivative acquisition

§ 4. The System of Transfer of Ownership

1. Introduction

With the introduction of the Civil Code German law has parted from the old transfer system of *titulus* and *modus* provided for by the German '*Gemeines Recht*' (literally: common law). Strongly influednced by the theory of legal acts by *Friedrich von Savigny*,[1] it was replaced by the abstract transfer system.
Starting point of the German transfer system is, somewhat simplified, that a legal consequence can either follow directly from a statutory provision or from a party's legal act. As the law – different than the French Code Civil – does not grant the contractual agreement translatory effect, the legal consequence, *i.e.* the transfer of title, must find its basis in an agreement distinct from the obligation created by the parties. The basis of the transfer therefore is held to be the agreement on the transfer of title, this real agreement being an agreement *in rem*.[2] Furthermore, this agreement must be made public by *traditio*, that is the transfer of possession. As far as these requirements are fulfilled all powers embraced in the right of ownership pass to the transferee *uno actu*. This effect of transfer is mandatory and can consequently not be altered by agreement.[3]
The transfer of title is a consequence of the real agreement, not of the obligatory agreement. Therefore the obligatory act as the underlying justification for the legal transaction has lost its importance for the transfer of title: the cause in law as the economic justification for the transfer is reduced to an underlying rationale of the transfer, but is no longer a requirement for its validity. Consequently a potential invalidity of the contractual agreement does not have any detrimental effect on the validity of the real agreement. It does not render the transfer of title invalid.
Also the type of the underlying obligation is without relevance: contractual as extra-contractual obligations merely give rise to a claim for transfer of title, but can neither substitute the real agreement nor the transfer. Even a claim recognized by declaratory judgment stating that the claimant is entitled to acquire ownership

---

[1] Cf. *Brehm/Berger*, Sachenrecht (2000), no. 26.8.

[2] By contrast *Savigny* regarded the agreement *in rem* as a real contract and similarly the first draft of the German Civil Code has followed this approach, *Brehm/Berger*, Sachenrecht (2000), no. 26.8 ff.

[3] An exception is made with respect to security interest by transfer of title: in case of insolvency of the secured creditor it is taken into account that the legal position exceeds the allocation of property from an economical point of view (cf. *infra § 8*).

does only constitute a valid cause and therefore creates an obligation of the owner to transfer ownership.[4]

The consequence of this abstract transfer system is that the determination of ownership is exclusively answered according to the provisions of property law and without regard to the underlying obligatory cause.

2. The Concept of the Abstract Nature of Rights *in rem*

As mentioned above German law has adopted the abstract transfer system and thereby presupposes the distinction between obligatory agreement and real agreement (*Trennungsprinzip*). This indicates that the transfer is not a result of the contractual agreement, but requires a distinct real agreement.[5] The validity of obligatory agreement and real agreement have to be determined separately.[6]

The principle that rights *in rem* are of an abstract nature and independent of a legal cause has two aspects. The first is whether the real agreement requires a cause as justifying purpose and is referred to as material independence (*inhaltliche Abstraktion*). The second is whether the validity of the real agreement is dependant on the validity of the obligatory agreement, and is referred to as formal independence (*äußerliche Abstraktion*). The answer to both of this questions under German property law is clear-cut: the real agreement is free of any determination of purpose and therefore completely independent of the underlying cause.[7] This independence is supposed to promote legal certainty and clarity, as any doubts on the underlying cause and its validity do not affect the determination of property rights.[8] With this distinction German law has adopted the legal concept of *Savigny*:

This abstract transfer system may be characterised by its two most important consequences:

First, the conclusion of a contractual agreement which obliges a party to transfer title to another does in itself not affect the property right of the obligor. The creditor, that is the transferee does only acquire an obligatory claim for the conclusion of a respective real agreement. Thus for instance in the case of double

---

[4] Though the transferor's declaration of transfer of title can be replaced by a judgment (§ 894 ZPO).

[5] *Baur/Stürner*, Sachenrecht[17], § 51 no. 1.

[6] *Larenz/Wolf*, Schuldrecht AT, § 23 no. 78 ff.

[7] *Baur/Stürner*, Sachenrecht[17], § 5 no. 42.

[8] *Baur/Stürner*, Sachenrecht[17], § 5 no. 4; but cf. *Brehm/Berger*, Sachenrecht (2000), no. 1.22, who emphasize that the idea to further legal certainty has been a later justification but not the original intention.

sale both contractual agreements are perfectly valid, however, the seller is unable to fulfil both obligations (cf. *infra § 6*).[9]
Second, the real agreement is considered to be ‚neutral' and therefore is held to be valid even in case the underlying contract is void, for instance, because it is contrary to law or *boni mores*. However, this consequence has often been criticised and some exceptions have been accepted.[10]

3. The Valid Obligation

a) Obligations Transfer of Ownership Can Be Based On

The question on what kind of obligations transfer of title may be based on is difficult to answer from a German law perspective. The correct answer would probably be: any kind or even none at all. Due to the abstract transfer system the transfer will be evenly valid even in case there is no underlying obligation. The question therefore has to be modified: what kind of obligation can a transfer of title be based on to achieve the result that the legal order lastingly accepts the new allocation of goods?
As a general rule transfer of title can be based on any kind of obligation, which obliges one party to transfer a property right to the other party. These can be a contract imposing mutual obligations (*e.g.* sale or barter), gratuitous contracts (*e.g.* a gift) or may arise from an extra-contractual obligation (*e.g.* delict, unjustified enrichment, benevolent intervention). Similarly a unilateral legal transaction (*i.e.* promise of a reward) may form the legal cause for the subsequent transfer or title. The type of obligation does not have any immediate effect on the transfer.
On the other hand, the legal order has to take into account that the different types of obligations are of varying strength with regard to their ability to justify the result of the transfer, *i.e.* the right of the transferee to keep the property transferred. As a consequence of the abstract transfer system a direct influence with respect to transfer of title is not acknowledged. But a differentiation is drawn with regard to the question whether or not the transferee is obliged to retransfer the property acquired. In this context it is self-evident that a person who has received a thing as a gift is not worthy of the same protection which is afforded to a person who acquired property by means of counter-performance. Although this

[9] The mere fact that the transferee knows of the sale to another person does not in itself constitute a defect of the real agreement, unless is constitutes a wilful damage contrary to public policy (§ 826), *infra § 6*.
[10] As to these modifications of the abstract transfer system cf. *infra § 4 3. c*.

distinction of course is not drawn within the rules on property law, the legal technique should be illustrated by an example.
A sells an asset to B and transfers it to him. B subsequently makes the asset a gift to C. Afterwards, A discovers that the sales contract with B was void (for example due to a formal defect). As the contractual agreement between A and B is void, the valid transfer of title lacks a valid cause as its justification. B is unjustly enriched and therefore obliged to retransfer the asset according to § 812 subsection 1. However, B is unable to retransfer the asset as he has in the meantime transferred ownership to C. The obligation to retransfer property therefore is replaced by a duty to transfer whatever he has obtained in place of the asset originally transferred. As B has not received anything in return for his gift, A could neither claim retransfer nor the substitute. Yet, C who has obtained the asset without consideration is not equally worthy of protection as A. § 822 therefore provides that C has to transfer the asset to A.
A similar distinction between acquisition for consideration and gratuitous acquisition is provided for in the context of *bona fide*-acquisition. In case the third party has *bona fide* acquired ownership, other provisions that grant a claim for retransfer to the former owner (arising from tort law or unjustified enrichment) are as a general rule excluded. Again an exception is made for the case the acquirer has obtained property without consideration (§ 816 subsection 1 sentence 2).

> **§ 816 [Disposition by Unauthorized Person]**
>
> (1) If an unauthorized person disposes of an object and this disposition is effective towards the entitled person, the unauthorized person is obliged to give up what he obtained by the disposition to the entitled person. If the disposition was gratuitous, the same obligation lies on the person who obtained a legal advantage immediately by the disposition.

Similarly a transfer is of course also valid in case there is no underlying cause at all.[11] However, the acquirer will in general be unjustly enriched and therefore obliged to retransfer ownership according to § 812 ff.

b) Consequences of Defects of the Obligation on the Transfer of Ownership

The reasons why a contractual agreement may be void or avoidable are to be found in the General Part of the Civil Code (First Book). A first source of defects is the lack of legal capacity to enter into legal transactions according to § 104 ff. For example a declaration of will made by a person underage is void, the contractual agreement therefore ineffective. The same consequence is also

[11] Cf. *Jauernig*, JuS 1994, 721.

provided for in case a declaration is subject to a mental reservation made to a person, who is aware of that reservation (§ 116), the declaration of intention made only in pretence (§ 117) or a declaration lacking seriousness, which is made in the expectation that the lack of seriousness is discovered (§ 118). A contract may further be void in case it suffers a defect of form required by statute (§ 125), as is a contract, which is contrary to law (§ 134) or contrary to fundamental principles of morality (§ 138).

Other defects of the declaration of intention as a general rule make the contract avoidable. Thus the contract is valid unless and until it is avoided by the party entitled to claim avoidance.[12] The most important applications are the error as to the content of the declaration made or the lack of intention to make a declaration (§ 119), the incorrect transmission of a declaration of intention (§ 120) and finally the declaration of intention under the influence of fraud or duress (§ 123).

By contrast, an error about the solvency of the contracting partner is not accepted as a reason to claim avoidance, unless the creditor has been fraudulently mislead on this point in the meaning of § 123. In case the contracting partner is unable to meet his obligation the only remedy granted to the creditor is to revoke the contract on the reason of lack of performance (§ 323). The same holds true, if he has performed in advance without reservation of title, as the defective performance does not have any effect on the validity of transfer. The executed consideration may be reclaimed under § 326 subsection 4 in accordance with §§ 346 ff.

As mentioned above a lack of legal capacity, the contract being void or avoidable for reason of error, fraud or duress does not constitute a defect of the real agreement (unless the latter itself is defective for the same reason). Even the fact that the contractual agreement is subject to a condition on itself does not affect the real agreement, unless it is similarly subject to a condition. The acquirer therefore may acquire ownership despite an invalid or conditional contract. Exceptions from this rule are only acknowledged to a very narrow extent (on this cf. *infra c*).

Of course the validity of the real agreement cannot change the fact that the transfer of property does lack an economic justification. The considerations executed therefore have to be retransferred according to the rules on unjustified enrichment (§§ 812 ff.). The retransfer follows the general rules, *i.e.* it consists of a real agreement and a *traditio*. The underlying cause for retransfer is the claim *ex* unjustified enrichment.

The necessity of a formal retransfer *ex* unjustified enrichment leads to the consequence that until such retransfer the acquirer is the legal owner and is authorized to dispose of the property. He can accordingly transfer it to any third party, who in turn acquires from an authorized transferor. In case the transferee

[12] Hk-BGB/*Dörner*, § 142 no. 3.

due to such further subsequent transfer is unable to retransfer the asset he has to compensate the value. In case the transferee in the mean-time has declared insolvency, the transferor (*i.e.* the former owner) is even worse off: whereas a causal system would grant him a revindication, the abstract system substitutes this by a claim for a percentage in insolvency (cf. *infra § 8)*.

c) Exceptions From the System of Abstract Tradition

The general rule set out above is that the real agreement is not affected by a defective contractual agreement and that in consequence considerations already executed are reclaimed *ex* unjustified enrichment and not revindicated. However, this rule has not remained without exceptions. [13]

Such exceptions from the principle of abstract tradition have been acknowledged in three different categories of cases: As contractual agreement and real agreement both are subject to the same rules of the General Part (First Book) defects such as a lack of legal capacity may similarly affect the real agreement of its own right and lead to an identity of defect (so-called *Fehleridentität*). Second, the assessment of the contractual agreement as contrary to statute law or *boni mores* may lead to the result that the economic result of the real agreement were unbearable (so-called *Gesetz- or Sittenwidrigkeit*). Third, the defect of the contractual agreement may affect the real agreement if this is in line with the (presumed) intention of the parties (*Geschäftseinheit*).

aa) Identical Defect of Contractual and Real Agreement

The real agreement is subject to the same provisions of the General Part as the contractual agreement. Thus, a defect such as lack of legal capacity cannot only affect the contractual agreement but may also affect the real agreement. In case both agreements suffer the same defect this is commonly called identity of defects (*Fehleridentität*).

Although this category of cases is commonly referred to as an exception from the principle of abstract tradition, it is not in the strict sense an alteration of the principle of independence of the agreement *in rem* from the obligatory cause. For the reason for the defect of the real agreement is not the defect of the obligatory cause. Instead the link between these two agreements consists merely in the coincidence that the same fact which has rendered the obligatory cause ineffective leads to a similar defect of the real agreement.[14] That there is no dependence of the defect of one agreement on the defect of the other is apparent in case the

[13] This is criticised by *Jauernig*, JuS 1994, 721, 723 ff.

[14] *Rinne* in: MünchKomm BGB^4 VI, Introduction, no. 19; *Jauernig*, JuS 1994, 721, 724.

defect is cured between the conclusion of the contractu and conclusion of the real agreement: if for instance one contracting party in the meantime reaches the age of 18 and thereby full legal capacity, then the real agreement is valid because it meets the requirements of an agreement under the rules of the General Part. The mere fact that the obligatory agreement remains invalid does not affect the transfer of title.
In this context it should be mentioned, that although contractual agreement and real agreement both are subject to the same rules of the General Part, this does not automatically lead to the result, that the examination of the validity of each of the agreements always has to correspond. A simple sale contract provides a good example. The contractual agreement obliging a minor to transfer title – the purchase price – to another is disadvantageous and therefore void. By contrast the transfer of ownership of the good to the minor is usually a declaration whereby he does merely acquire a legal benefit. By virtue of § 107 it is valid without consent of the representative. Thus the contractual agreement void, whereas the real agreement on the transfer of the 'purchased' goods is valid.
A further exception to the *Abstraktionsprinzip* is contained in the §§ 1365 f. and § 1369 on matrimonial property rights: unless the other spouse consents to the contractual agreement the subsequent real agreement is rendered void.[15]

bb) Contracts Contrary to Law or Contra *Boni Mores*

The independence of the real agreement from the underlying obligation in some cases may lead to the situation that the legal order would sanction a transfer or property, although it holds the obligation to be void due to its lack of conformity with fundamental principles of the legal order. If this is the case it is acknowledged that notwithstanding the nature of real agreements as ‚neutral', the legal order has to protect its values and in consequence let the defect of the contractual agreement extend to the real agreement.
Whether or not a statutory prohibition affects only the contractual agreement or extends to the real agreement is left to be determined according to the spirit and purpose of the statute.[16] The exact details of this requirement are – unsurprisingly – a matter of dispute.
Examples in which the defect of the contractual agreement has also rendered the 'neutral' real agreement void are the violation of a statutory prohibition in the meaning of § 134, which extends to the fulfilment of the real agreement[17] and the avoidance of the contract under § 123 (fraud and duress).[18] As far as usury under

[15] For details see *Wolf*, JZ 1997, 1087 ff.
[16] BGHZ 115, 123, 130; BGH NJW 1992, 2349, 2350; Staudinger/*Wiegand* (2004), § 929 no. 21.
[17] BGHZ 1, 128, 131; BGHZ 115, 123, 130; BGHZ 122, 115, 122.
[18] *Baur/Stürner*, Sachenrecht[17], § 5 no. 51.

§ 138 subsection 2 is concerned, the real agreement transferring property to the usurer is void for the benefit of the exploited person.[19]

If by contrast merely the contractual agreement is contrary to fundamental principles of morality under § 138 subsection 1, the general rule is that the real agreement is ‚morally neutral'.[20] Thus it does not come within the scope of identical defect of contractual and real agreement[21] mentioned above. The retransfer of executed performance instead again follows the rules of § 812 ff.[22] Only in exceptional cases the lack of conformity with *boni mores* may arise from the purpose and result of the real agreement.[23] Here the 'neutral' real agreement is scrutinized on its substance according to the same criteria the contractual agreement has to meet.[24] An example for a real agreement that fails to meet this standard may be a fiduciary transfer if the economic activity of the party furnishing security thereby is unduly restricted or other creditors are discriminated.[25] This for example applies in case of delay to declare bankruptcy,[26] excessive securities for a debt[27] or misguidance to breach of contract by means of a general assignment of all rights and claims.[28]

cc) Stipulation of Conditions and Partial Nullity

The real agreement may be concluded subject to conditions inserted by the parties. Such conditions may be both conditions precedent and conditions subsequent. Thus the parties can as a general rule agree that the validity of the real agreement shall depend on the validity of the contractual agreement.[29] A further requirement of such conditions, which may be also agreed upon tacitly, is that the parties at the time of conclusion are in doubt of whether or not the requirement

---

[19] BGH NJW 1982, 2767; cf. Staudinger/*Wiegand* (2004), § 929 no. 21 with further references.

[20] BGH NJW 1973, 613, 615; BGH NJW 1990, 385; *Jauernig*, JuS 1994, 721, 725.

[21] Staudinger/*Wiegand* (2004), § 929 no. 21; Hk-BGB/*Dörner*, § 138 no. 16.

[22] Hk-BGB/*Dörner*, § 138 no. 16.

[23] *Baur/Stürner*, Sachenrecht[17], § 5 no. 51; this proposition is, however, rejected by judicature in the majority of cases, cf. BGH NJW 1985, 3007; BGH NJW 1988, 2364; BGH NJW-RR 1989, 519; BGH NJW 1992, 593, 594.

[24] *Wiegand*, AcP 190 (1990), 113, 124.

[25] *Baur/Stürner*, Sachenrecht[17], § 5 no. 51.

[26] BGH NJW 1995, 1668.

[27] BGHZ 7, 111; BGHZ 10, 228; BGHZ 19, 13, 18; BGH NJW 1998, 671. The judicature, however, has subsequently departed from the original line of holding excessive securities to be contrary to *boni mores*, cf. BGH NJW 1991, 354; NJW 1991, 2147; NJW 1996, 2786.

[28] BGH NJW 1991, 2147; BGH NJW 1995, 1668, 1669.

[29] Whereas the transfer of immovables has to be unconditional, § 925 subsection 2.

will be fulfilled. Otherwise the acceptance of a perhaps tacitly agreed condition precedent may lead to a circumvention of the principle of abstract tradition.[30]
The possibility to make the validity of the transfer of ownership depend on a stipulated condition is for example made use of for the construction of a reservation of title. However, in this case the validity of the real agreement is not subject to the condition that the contractual agreement is valid, but instead to the complete payment of the purchase price. Therefore the concept of reservation is no alteration of the principle of formal independence, but it clearly demonstrates that a real agreement may be conditional.
A similar alteration or rather exception from the abstract transfer system may be effected by virtue of the rule on partial nullity comprised in § 139. This provision contains a legal presumption that in case one part of a legal transaction is void the whole legal transaction is void, unless it may be assumed that it would have been entered into even if the void part had been omitted. According to the prevailing opinion § 139 is not only applicable to several parts of one legal transaction but also to a unity of separate transactions. Whether or not this also may be extended to a unity of contractual and real agreement is a matter of controversy.
As an argument against such application it is brought forward, that the abstract transfer system has given the interest of legal certainty of third parties preference over the interest of the parties to secure the result sought.[31] According to this opinion the application of the rule on partial nullity in this case would operate contrary to the core of the abstract transfer system and hence may not be applied[32] or at least only subject to very narrow exceptions.[33] Other authors have argued in favour of the application of the rule on partial nullity as a link between contractual agreement and real agreement. Thus they argue that the abstract transfer system is not mandatory, but subject to the disposition of the parties.[34] The prevailing opinion disagrees and holds fast to the mandatory nature.[35] Despite this prevailing opinion in legal doctrine the judicature has in various cases applied § 139 to cases

---

[30] *Baur/Stürner*, Sachenrecht[17], § 5 no. 53; *Brehm/Berger*, Sachenrecht (2000), no. 1.27; *Jauernig*, JuS 1994, 721, 723.
[31] *Baur/Stürner*, Sachenrecht[17], § 5 no. 56 with reference to BayObLG Rpfleger 1969, 48; this line of argument may also be traced in the decisions BGH NJW 1979, 1496, BGH NJW 1985, 3007; BGH NJW 1988, 2364; BGH NJW-RR 1992, 593, 954.
[32] *Quack* in: MünchKomm BGB[4] VI, § 929 no. 71.
[33] *Rinne* in: MünchKomm BGB[4] VI, Introduction, no. 18; *Brehm/Berger*, Sachenrecht (2000), no. 1.26.; *Jauernig*, JuS 1994, 721, 724.
[34] *Heck*, Grundriß des Sachenrechts (1930), 121 ff.; Staudinger/*Seiler* (2000), Introduction to Property Law, no. 50; Staudinger/*Wiegand* (2004), Introduction to § 929 no. 18, § 929 no. 27; *Eisenhardt*, JZ 1991, 271, 277; *Wiegand*, AcP 190 (1990), 135.
[35] *Mayer-Maly/Busche* in: MünchKomm BGB[4] I, § 139 no. 16; *Rinne* in: MünchKomm BGB[4] VI, Introduction, no. 18; Staudinger/*Roth* (2000), § 139 BGB no. 54.

where the contractual agreement was void and has consequently held the real agreement to be similarly void.[36]

4. The Real Agreement

The strict distinction between the law of obligations and property law has lead to an independence of the transfer of title: it is no longer understood to be the fulfilment of the contractual agreement but instead a self-standing legal transaction. Thus the Civil Code in the two central provisions on derivative acquisition of ownership (§§ 873, 929) introduces the requirement of a real agreement, that is an agreement between transferor and transferee on the sole subject of transfer of title. This agreement is a contract *in rem* and therefore a particular emanation of a transaction *in rem*.

This sophisticated distinction between contractual agreement on the underlying cause and the real agreement restricted to the transfer has repeatedly been criticized by leading legal scholars.[37] It has in particular been emphasized that the rationale of legal security and certainty of third parties can already be achieved by application of the rules on *bona fide*-acquisition as set out in § 932 ff. The abstract transfer system therefore were rendered superfluous. However, it has to be emphasized that the prevailing opinion in legal doctrine, as the unanimous judicature, does not challenge the concept of an abstract transfer system.[38]

The requirement of a real agreement (*Einigung*) on the transfer of ownership in movables is expressly set out in § 929 1st sentence, but reaches beyond this provision. It is applicable also to the subsequent transfer modes of § 929 2nd sentence, § 929a, § 930 and § 931, as for the *bona fide*-acquisition under §§ 932 ff. The latter only modify the requirement of *traditio*.

5. The Concept of Transfer of Possession

a) General Rule and Exceptions

The principle of distinction between obligatory cause and real agreement (*Trennungsprinzip*) is a prerequisite for the existence of a separate real agreement, but it in itself does not yet answer the question whether the transfer of title is effected by consensus alone or does in addition need a transfer of possession (*traditio*). It would be similarly possible that the conclusion of the real agreement

---

[36] Cf. RGZ 57, 96; RGZ 153, 352; BGH NJW 1967, 1128, 1130; BGH NJW 1986, 2642; BGHZ 31, 321, 323; see also BGHZ 38, 187, 193 (*obiter*).

[37] Cf. *Larenz*, Schuldrecht BT II § 39 II d; *H. Westermann*, Lehrbuch des Sachenrechts^6, § 4 III.

[38] For details see *Stadler*, Gestaltungsfreiheit und Verkehrsschutz durch Abstraktion (1996), 76 ff.

by itself already effects the transfer of ownership. Such a system – it has been argued – may even better match the idea of abstract transfer, as the transfer of possession originally was considered to constitute the fulfilment of the contractual agreement.[39] However, the Civil Code has held on to the requirement of *traditio*. The transfer of possession though is not considered as the fulfilment of the contractual agreement, but instead as a means of publicity. It is a substitute for the entry of the transfer in immovables into the land register.
Turning to the underlying rationale of the principle of *traditio* we have to take into account that the transfer requirement fulfils a different purpose in case of transfer from an authorized person in contrast to *bona fide*-acquisition from an unauthorized person.[40] We shall first turn to the purpose of *traditio* in case of transfer by an authorized transferor.
In case of transfer from an authorized person the transfer requirement serves as the fulfilment of the real agreement. It thereby serves legal certainty as a change of property rights only takes place where an actual act of transfer takes place.[41] Lacking this requirement there would be an imminent danger, that the distribution of liability is circumvented by means of a sham transfer of title. The owner of assets about to be seized could easily assert that he has long since transferred property to a third party. This concept is often referred to as the function of reliability (*Seriositätsfunktion*), (cf. *supra § 1 3. c*).[42]
The principle of *traditio* is expressed by the requirement of transfer of possession in § 929 1st sentence: the real agreement must be completed by a factual element, which as a general rule will be the transfer of physical control over the asset disposed of from the transferor to the transferee.
If this requirement of transfer of physical control were strict then the transaction by an owner, who does not have direct possession of the asset he intends to dispose of would always require the owner to first obtain direct possession.[43] The consequence were that an asset which is subject to – for instance – a lease contract could not be sold, as the lessee is by virtue of the contract entitled to direct possession. He has a valid defence against the owner's claim for recovery (cf. § 986). The strict adherence to the principle of *traditio* may in some cases also lead to an unnecessary double transfer.

---

[39] Cf. *Brehm/Berger*, Sachenrecht (2000), no. 26.12
[40] *Brehm/Berger*, Sachenrecht (2000), no. 26.11.
[41] *Brehm/Berger*, Sachenrecht (2000), no. 26.12
[42] *Brehm/Berger*, Sachenrecht (2000), no. 26.12. This concern about the conclusion of sham real agreements is one of the reasons why the transfer mode of constructive possession in § 930 requires a specified relationship of indirect possession (cf. Motive III, 98 ff. and *supra § 2 2. a)*. this has even been interpreted as a restriction of the abstract transfer system: because the fulfilment of the real agreement will in most cases at the same time be the fulfilment of the contractual obligation, despite the fact that an underlying cause is no longer required (loc.cit.).
[43] Cf. *Brehm/Berger*, Sachenrecht (2000), no. 26.13.

The law reacts to these difficulties by dispensing from the *traditio* requirement in case the transferee already has possession (§ 929 2nd sentence) or does permit the *traditio* to be substituted by other transfer modes (§ 930 and § 931). The modes of actual transfer (or of the respective substitute modes that may replace actual transfer) set out in §§ 929 ff. are exclusive: actual transfer (§ 929 1st sentence), *brevi manu traditio* (§ 929 2nd sentence), *constitutum possessorium* (§ 930) and assignment of the claim for recovery (§ 931). All modes have in common that the transferee must obtain some form of physical control, *i.e.* at least indirect possession.[44]

However, even with regard to the mentioned substitute modes provided for, the strict adherence to the *traditio* principle would lead to consequences, which are contrary to the needs of modern business transactions.[45] As an example a chain of delivery would be impossible, because the delivery from the manufacturer directly to the end-consumer would not meet the respective transfer requirements. Delivery would instead have to take place from the manufacturer to the grossist, and from the latter to the retail seller etc. on to the end-consumer. Judicature and legal doctrine have reacted to this problem and have accepted the so-called *Geheißerwerb* as an additional substitute transfer mode.

By virtue of the *Geheißerwerb* transfer within each single limb of the delivery chain is construed, notwithstanding that the individual limbs of the delivery chain neither acquire direct possession, nor indirect possession by virtue of the *Geheißperson*. For the latter is not an intermediary possessor. The '*Geheißperson*' instead is a person, who has accepted the direction of another and acts accordingly. The possession of the respective transferee as the legitimatizing appearance therefore is replaced by the submission of the *Geheißperson* to the directions of the respective transferor.

We have seen above that the principle of *traditio* has found a considerable number of exceptions in the context of transfer of movables according to § 929 ff.[46] As far as acquisition from an unauthorized transferor is concerned the transfer requirement is more strictly adhered to.

This can be clearly seen in the transfer mode of § 932 subsection 1 2nd sentence, which corresponds to § 929 2nd sentence, but adds a further requirement, namely that the transferee must obtain possession *from* the transferor. Similarly § 930, which is the equivalent to § 933, requires transfer *by* the transferor. In case the transferor was neither owner nor direct possessor the transfer mode of assignment of claim for recovery requires that the transferee actually obtains direct possession from the third party. In all these cases, the further requirement of actual transfer serves the protection of the owner, as the requirements cannot be met, *i.e.* he

---

[44] See on the concept of *Geheißerwerb*, *infra § 5 4. c)*.
[45] *Brehm/Berger*, Sachenrecht (2000), no. 26.12.
[46] *Baur/Stürner*, Sachenrecht[17], § 51 no. 3.

cannot be deprived of ownership, unless he has in some way made a contribution:[47] the minimum requirement is that he has handed over his asset to a third party, as a *bona fide*-acquisition will otherwise be excluded by § 935 (cf. *infra § 11*).

b) Restriction of Party Autonomy

The fact that the transfer principle has '*never been adhered to with consequence*'[48] or that judicature and legal doctrine in any case do allow exceptions, however, may not be interpreted as opening the door for party autonomy. The parties are not free to contract out of the transfer requirement. Here, as in the context of property law in general, the party autonomy with respect to form and content of transactions is severely restricted and in fact reduced to a choice between different transfer modes provided for by law. Other modes of transfer not set out in § 929 ff. are permissible only as far as acknowledged by judicature and legal doctrine.
Modifications by agreement of the parties, however, are permissible in respect to the real agreement. As an example the time of transfer can be agreed upon or can be made subject to a condition subsequent or precedent. Agreement and transfer of possession do not have to take place at the same time. For instance the agreement on transfer of title can by means of an anticipated *constitutum possessorium* already be concluded before the transferor himself has even acquired ownership.

c) Problems, Inconsistencies and Critique

The increasing tendency to accept exceptions from the *traditio* rule and the resulting discrepancy between the call for application of the transfer principle as for the principle of publicity, on the one hand, and the acceptance of substitute transfer modes developed by legal practice, on the other hand, have been criticized by legal doctrine. The critique in particular concerns the problem that the concept of possession as a means of publicity falls short of its equivalent in immovables, the land register. Thus the presumption of ownership in favour of the possessor contained in § 1006 due to acceptance of granting credit securities without actual transfer of possession in practice increasingly lacks a factual basis. The principle of *traditio* is further in particular affected by the acceptance of the transfer mode of *Geheißerwerb* in addition to those set out by the Civil Code.[49]

---

[47] *Brehm/Berger*, Sachenrecht (2000), no. 26.16.
[48] *Brehm/Berger*, Sachenrecht (2000), no. 26.12.
[49] Cf. *Quack* in: MünchKomm BGB^4 VI, § 929 no. 146.

For the *Geheißerwerb* only lives up to the reliability criterion contained in the principle of *traditio*, but does not pay heed to the principle of publicity.[50]
However, while scholars are unanimous with regard to the description of the problem, the conclusions drawn and the opinions on the proper solution are wide-ranging:
The various exceptions have led *Heck* to the statement that the transfer principle represents the general rule, but does not constitute a mandatory rule. Therefore the parties were free to transfer ownership by mere agreement.[51]
By contrast *Quack* argues that the provisions of the Civil Code can be adopted to the necessities of modern business transactions and communication. Thus, it should not be held fast to the transfer requirement. Instead the transfer requirement should be construed as the requirement of a two-stage transfer. The second stage, that is transfer, could easily be replaced by a legal transaction.[52]
Similarly *Wiegand* points out the superiority of the reliability criterion over publicity, a preference, which he argues has already been the main focus of the legislator. Therefore, the transfer requirement could be widely interpreted: the sole requirement were that the change of ownership leads to some change of possession, without further distinction whether this change of possession is brought about by the owner, a direct or indirect possessor or a *Geheißperson*.[53]
Other authors, however, argue in favour of return to the principle of publicity. For instance *Larenz* has proposed to return to the old system of an underlying contract and *traditio*, as it was foreseen by the *Allgemeines Landrecht* (ALR). The *traditio* requirement would remain in place, whereas the distinction between obligatory cause and real agreement would be relinquished.[54] *Wacke* has plead in favour of this distinction, but for the abandonment of the abstract transfer system.[55] *Baur/Stürner* have emphasized the importance of the principle of publicity, but propose to adapt it to the necessities of business transactions by creating a register for movables as an alternative to transfer of possession.[56]
All in all, there seems to be a preponderance of votes in favour of the principle of *traditio*,[57] even more so, as in many works of authority the principle is not even a matter of discussion. Though this adherence to the principle of *traditio* according

---

[50] *Brehm/Berger*, Sachenrecht (2000), no. 27.32.
[51] *Heck* , Grundriss des Sachenrechts (1930), § 56.
[52] *Quack* in: MünchKomm BGB^4 VI, § 929 no. 146.
[53] Staudinger/*Wiegand* (2004), § 929 no. 55 ff.
[54] *Larenz*, Schuldrecht BT II/1 § 39 II d.
[55] *Wacke*, ZEuP 2000, 254, 257, yet he holds the abstract transfer system to be superfluous, loc. cit, 57.
[56] *Baur/Stürner*, Sachenrecht^{17}, § 51 no. 44; *Stürner*, JZ 1996, 741, 745 f.; see also *Grunsky*, JuS 1984, 497.
[57] *Baur/Stürner*, Sachenrecht^{17}, § 51 no. 4; *Larenz*, Schuldrecht BT II § 39 II d; see also the criticism by *Canaris*, FS Flume 1978, 372, 412.

to *Berger/Brehm* is merely a consequence of the fact ‚*that no clear rules can be derived from the principle and therefore it does not force to draw any consequences.*'[58] Similarly *Musielak* states that the principle of *traditio* in § 929 ff. has found such meagre expression that it may well be disputed, if it should be at all counted among the general principles of property law.[59]

6. Registration

As mentioned above German property law only provides for two means of publicity, namely transfer of possession and entry into the land register. The only exception to this rule is provided for in respect of ships. Although a movable asset the principle of publicity is adhered to by means of registration in a specific ship register.
The rules on this ship register are not contained in the Civil Code, but are the subject of separate statute on registered ships and ship-yards (*Gesetz über Rechte an eingetragenen Schiffen und Schiffsbauwerken 1940*). This statute has replaced the former rule that pledge on a ship requires actual delivery to the pledgee. Instead it provides for pledge by registration in the ship register. This serves the possibility to 'split' ownership rights into security rights and rights to use and enjoy property.
The ship register is modelled after the land register. Ships beyond a stated size may be registered. As far as such a ship is registered, transfer of ownership follows rules similar to those on transfer of immovables. In case it is not registered, whether because it is too small or a registration has been omitted, the rules on transfer of title in movables apply (§ 929a and § 932a).
Leaving these specific rules aside, German law does not provide for registration of movable property. Yet, the introduction of such a register on movables has frequently been called for,[60] in order to replace the accepted credit securities lacking publicity.

---

58 *Brehm/Berger*, Sachenrecht (2000) no. 26.10.
59 *Musielak*, JuS 1992, 713, 716.
60 Cf. *Baur/Stürner*, Sachenrecht[17], § 52 no. 44.

§ 5. The Transfer Requirements with Respect to Movable Property

1. Overview on Transfer Requirements

The general rule for the transfer of title in movables is set out in the first sentence of § 929:

> **§ 929 BGB [Agreement and Delivery]:**
>
> For the transfer of ownership of a movable thing, it is necessary that the owner of the thing deliver it to the acquirer and that both agree that the ownership be transferred. [...]

This transfer mode is not only designed as the general rule but also is the most important in practice. It requires a real agreement and the transfer of possession. The disposition *in rem* therefore consists of two stages, namely the agreement as a contract on the change of rights *in rem* and a means of publicity. The sole content of the real agreement is the transfer of ownership; it is therefore 'neutral' or 'abstract' in the sense that it does not bear any reference to the underlying justification for the allocation of assets. The real agreement has to be completed by a transfer of possession to the transferee. The order of the two stages is without significance.[61] A further requirement of § 929 is not expressly set out, but tacitly comprised: the authority of the transferor to dispose.

The legislator of the year 1900 of course mainly had the actual transfer of physical control in view. Legal doctrine however has accepted, that this transfer mode is not sufficient for modern business transactions and has solved the problem by raising the requirements to a more abstract level. According to the prevailing opinion, the transfer under § 929 1st sentence has to meet the following requirements: (i) acquisition of possession of the transferee, (ii) loss of possession of the transferor and (iii) the new allocation of assets has to be covered by the will of the transferor and executed on the basis of the real agreement.

All subsequent transfer modes are based on § 929 1st sentence, whereas the requirement of a real agreement in the meaning of § 929 1st sentence remains the same for all transfer modes, § 929 2nd sentence, § 930 and § 931 each modify the requirements of transfer or respectively replace actual transfer by a substitute transfer mode.

The same holds true for the transfer modes of *bona fide*-acquisition. Each of them is based on the general rule comprising real agreement and transfer. The §§ 932 - 934 each mirror one of the transfer modes of § 929 ff., but contain modifications which pose stricter requirements with respect to transfer of possession:[62] *bona*

[61] *Baur/Stürner*, Sachenrecht[17], § 5 no. 30.
[62] *Brehm/Berger*, Sachenrecht (2000), no. 26.15.

fide-acquisition is only possible, if an actual transfer of possession takes place or in case of § 934 at least indirect possession is transferred.

2. Authority to Dispose

As can be derived from a comparison of § 929 ff. with § 932 ff., the first set of rules require the authority of the transferor to dispose of the asset. Whether the basis of this authority is ownership or an authority granted by contractual agreement with the owner, or based in law (such as liquidator in bankruptcy; parents) is without relevance. Whereas by contrast in the context of *bona fide*-acquisition, the good faith in the transferor's authority to dispose is in general not protected.

3. Real agreement

a) Agreement *in rem*

The minimum content of the agreement *in rem* is the determination of the parties and the specification of the assets to be transferred.[63] The agreement does not require any specific form and can be either declared expressly or tacitly. Frequently the agreement *in rem* will coincide with the conclusion of the underlying contractual agreement, but nevertheless has to be distinguished from a legal point of view. In case the agreement *in rem* takes place considerable time after the contractual agreement and thus has not yet been tacitly included in the contractual agreement, the agreement can be – tacitly – implied in the transfer. As the real agreement is a contract it is necessarily bilateral.
As a contract *in rem* the real agreement is subject to the provisions of the General Part of the Civil Code (First Book), unless these general rules are prevailed over by specific property law rules.[64] The application of the General Part *inter alia* relates to legal capacity,[65] defects of declaration of intention, form of legal transactions, conclusion of contracts, construction of contracts[66] and the effect of a violation of statute.[67] As a disposition *in rem* the contract *in rem* further is subject to relative prohibitions of alienation (§§ 135, 136). The rules on obligations contained in the Second Book, by contrast, are not applicable.[68]

---

[63] *Quack* in: MünchKomm BGB[4] VI, § 929 no. 71.
[64] *Baur/Stürner*, Sachenrecht[17], § 5 no. 5.
[65] Cf. BGH NJW 1988, 3260; BGHZ 78, 28, 35.
[66] BGH WM 1978, 194.
[67] BGHZ 11, 59, 61; BGH NJW 1983, 636; BGHZ 115, 123, 130.
[68] *Baur/Stürner*, Sachenrecht[17], § 5 no. 25; BGHZ 49, 263, 264 ff.

The provisions on agency and grant of authority are equally applicable to real agreements:[69] The owner may authorize a third party to dispose of his property (§ 185 subsection 1) or can subsequently ratify a disposition performed by such person without prior consent (§ 185 subsection 2). This possibility is of major importance with respect to the extended reservation of title as for the fiduciary transfer of title; because both forms of credit securities are based on the possibility of the debtor to use and perhaps to resell the assets in order to earn the capital necessary to repay the loan.
The real agreement can be made subject to a condition or a time limit imposed. Thus the real agreement may be subject to a reservation of title, which contains the requirement of complete payment of the purchase price as a condition precedent (§ 449, cf. *infra § 13*).
Peculiarities of the real agreement in comparison to contractual agreements only exist insofar as the real agreement according to the prevailing opinion does not have a binding effect.[70] Instead it may freely be withdrawn.[71] Further the authority of the transferor is a prerequisite to the real agreement. Both requirements must be met at the point of time the two-staged transfer is completed, therefore at the time the second act is executed,[72] the order of agreement and transfer being exchangeable.

b) Clarity and Identification

As set out above, the principle of specificity requires a separate real agreement for each thing transferred, even in case the agreements on a variety of assets transferred are combined in a single declaration. The difference between the combination of various specific declarations and a summarized declaration is evident in case a variety of things is transferred, but an error giving a right to avoidance occurs only with respect to a single thing. Unless the rule on partial nullity under § 139 applies, the result is that the avoidance of the respective real agreement only leads to the invalidity of transfer of title concerning this specific asset, while the transfer with respect to the other assets remains valid.
A prerequisite of the real agreement therefore is that the parties agree on the object of the contract. To satisfy this requirement the assets to be transferred have

---

69 Agency is only available with respect to the real agreement, not for the transfer of possession, but may be replaced by the concept of transfer by intermediaries.

70 For contracts the binding effect is expressly provided for in § 145 ff.

71 BGHZ 14, 114, 122; BGH NJW 1978, 696; BGH NJW 1979, 213; of other opinion *H. Westermann*, vol. 1, § 38 4. Though the continuation of the real agreement is presumed, unless there are indications for the opposite: of other opinion *Brehm/Berger*, Sachenrecht (2000), no. 27.11. In case the transferor is obliged by contract to agree to transfer of title, he may be ordered by judgment to agree to transfer of title (§ 894 ZPO).

72 *Baur/Stürner*, Sachenrecht[17], § 51 no. 11.

to be specified beyond question at the time of the disposition. According to the judicature of the Federal Supreme Court it is sufficient, if an independent onlooker who has knowledge of the agreement, can determine which assets are covered by the agreement.[73] This determination must be complete at the time of execution of the transfer.[74] The fact that it may at a later stage be difficult to prove, whether or not a particular asset was covered by the transfer, is of no relevance in the context of specificity.[75] The judicature on this point in some respects is quite casuistic, though a tendency to reduce the standard can be made out.[76] The judicature has held the following specification to be sufficient:

- A stock in trade, with the additional declaration that the transferor in respect of some of the assets contained, but not further specified, only had conditional and not full ownership.[77]
- All assets stored in a particular room at the time of transfer.[78]
- All aggregate things stored in specific rooms of a warehouse, in which other assets were similarly stored, which did not belong to the aggregate assets.[79]

The following specifications were held to be insufficient

- The determination of the asset as part of a kind of assets[80]
- The specification as 75 fattened pigs, which were in fact held separately, because the separate keeping was not contained in the parties' agreement.[81]
- The determination by goods of a value or price up to the amount of a specified sum.[82]
- The agreement that all such assets are subject to the transfer, which are the property of the transferor.[83]

---

[73] This so-called 'onlooker-rule' (‚*Beobachterformel*') is consistent practice of the courts since BGHZ 73, 253, 254 f. See also BGH NJW 1984, 803; BGH NJW 1986, 1985; BGH NJW 1992, 1161; BGH NJW 1994, 133. For criticism see *Quack* in: MünchKomm BGB[4] VI, § 929 no. 78.

[74] *Quack* in: MünchKomm BGB[4] VI, § 929 no. 87.

[75] *Quack* in: MünchKomm BGB[4] VI, § 929 no. 87; *Brehm/Berger*, Sachenrecht (2000), no. 27.3.

[76] For criticism see *Baur/Stürner*, Sachenrecht[17], § 4 no. 19 and *Feuerborn*, ZIP 2001, 600, 602 ff.

[77] BGHZ 28, 16 (with explicit deviation from BGHZ 21, 52).

[78] *Quack* in: MünchKomm BGB[4] VI, § 929 no. 83.

[79] BGH ZIP 2000, 1895.

[80] BGHZ 21, 52.

[81] BGH NJW 1984, 803, 804; for criticism see *Gursky*, JZ 1991, 496, 498.

[82] BGHZ 21, 52, 55 (*obiter*).

[83] BGHZ 21, 52; insofar confirmed by BGHZ 28, 16, 20; BGH WM 1986, 594; see also *Quack* in: MünchKomm BGB[4] VI, § 929 no. 83.

- The agreement that half of the assets stored as stock-in-trade shall be transferred, because, having this agreement in mind, it cannot be specified for every single asset whether it belongs to the relevant half.

The reference to a future specification is similarly insufficient.[84] However, this defect can be cured by an anticipated agreement: in case the agreement takes place preceding the transfer it may refer to a thing, which does not yet exist or is not yet specified, and will take effect as soon as the thing comes into existence or is specified by segregation from the stock-in-trade. This possibility is of great practical importance in the context of credit security by fiduciary transfer, as this permits a transfer of a changing stock-in-trade: as soon as the assets are brought into the respective warehouse rooms they are at the same time specified and the real agreement takes effect (storage security contract)[85].

4. Tradition

a) General Rule

The general rule on transfer of title in movables is that a transfer based on a legal act needs a form of publicity (cf. *supra § 1 3. c*). This publicity requirement in the context of immovables is met by entry into the land register, in respect of movables by transfer of physical control (cf. *supra § 2 3. b*).
The basic transfer mode is contained in § 929 1st sentence, requiring delivery in addition to the real agreement. Delivery here stands for actual transfer of physical control from the transferor to the transferee. This requirement of delivery, however, is modified in the subsequent paragraphs. § 929 2nd sentence even dispenses with transfer because the transferee already has possession of the involved asset (*traditio brevi manu*). § 930 permits the substitution of actual transfer by agreement on constructive possession. The former owner remains in possession and agrees to hold it for the new owner as the indirect possessor (*constitutum possessorium*). § 932 finally replaces actual physical control by the assignment of the claim to recover possession (*traditio longa manu*). Thereby the transferee merely obtains indirect possession (cf. § 870).

b) The Aim of Correspondence Between Possession and Ownership

The purpose of the principle of publicity is to secure the conformity of possession and ownership and thereby restrict the possibility of dispositions of unauthorized persons. The underlying rationale is that unauthorized persons due to lack of

[84] BGH NJW 1991, 2144.
[85] Cf. BGHZ 117, 200.

possession cannot transfer possession and accordingly cannot transfer ownership.[86]

This underlying principle, however, has not been adopted by the Civil Code in such a stringent way as to correspond to this rationale: instead there are cases in which the owner can transfer ownership by mere agreement (*e.g.* in case a thief is the possessor of the thing). Other transfer modes allow transfer of ownership without requiring that the transferee obtains possession (*e.g.* the asset is handed over to a third party by a person under the direction of the transferor by means of a *Geheißerwerb*, cf. *infra c aa*).

Further the substitute transfer modes provided for in § 930 and 931 are legal transactions and not factual transactions, they therefore are not perceptible for third parties. They only conform to the principle of *traditio* insofar, as they transfer indirect possession to the transferee and therefore satisfy the reliability criterion, but do not comprise any publicity.

In order to satisfy the growing demand for flexibility of modern business transactions the purpose to secure the conformity of possession and ownership has been put last and accordingly the principle of publicity has increasingly been neglected.[87] This in particular becomes obvious in the case of a chain of delivery: the transfer of possession from one limb of the delivery chain to the next is a *traditio ficta*. The manufacturer in fact can deliver the goods straight to the end-consumer without the respective reseller ever setting hand on it.[88]

c) Forms of Tradition

The transfer of ownership in movables follows the principle of *traditio* and the principle of publicity. The first provides that the transfer mode as a rule is not executed before the real agreement is accompanied by an actual transfer of possession. Transfer of possession here means mutual transfer of direct possession. The principle of publicity states that such transfer of ownership shall be made known to third parties by an apparent change of possession. In spite of this general rule, the law does not strictly adhere to the principle of publicity, as it provides for transfer modes that allow to substitute the physical transfer by agreements and the change of possession thus remains undisclosed. Legal practice has developed even more exceptions from the principle of publicity. Yet, it is derived from the principle of *traditio* that the requirement of transfer is not a matter of party disposition.

The transfer modes provided for are generously construed, in particular with respect to the involvement of third parties in the act of transfer of possession. As

---

[86] *Brehm/Berger*, Sachenrecht (2000), no. 26.12.
[87] *Brehm/Berger*, Sachenrecht (2000), no. 26.12.
[88] *Brehm/Berger*, Sachenrecht (2000), no. 26.13.

the transfer of possession is a natural act – as opposed to a legal act – the rules on agency do not apply. This gap is filled by the concept of intermediaries, which may act in place of the transferor, as well as by the generally acknowledged concept of transfer by a *Geheißperson.*
The parties may freely choose between the different transfer modes, a specific justification why the parties chose the one over the other is not required. All transfer modes and substitute transfer modes are adequate. However, there is some divergence in the context of *bona fide*-acquisition (cf. *infra § 11 5.*).
Although the rules on transfer of movables in addition to the general rule contained in § 929 1st sentence only provide for three transfer modes, the modalities of valid transfer are manifold and confusing.[89] This may be best demonstrated by an example:[90]
A has lent a book to B. When A asks B to return the book, B is unable to find it. He does not know whether he has mislaid it at home or lent it to a third party or whether it even has been stolen. A and B therefore agree, that B compensates A for the value of the book and in case he finds it may keep the book in return. If B has merely mislaid the book in his apartment, he has acquired ownership according to § 929 2nd sentence. In case he has lost it, but later regains it this constitutes an anticipated real agreement under § 929 2nd sentence. In case A's daughter had the book at the time of the agreement, but later hands it over to B, B obtains ownership by virtue of 929 1st sentence. If the book finally has been stolen from B then B acquires ownership by assignment of the claim for recovery under § 931.
The different transfer modes therefore shall be set out separately according to the statutory order.

aa) Transfer of Ownership by Real Agreement and Delivery

A literal interpretation of § 929 1st sentence would require the transfer of direct possession immediately from the transferor to the transferee. However, this requirement is raised to a more abstract level of interpretation (cf. above *§ 4 5*) from which a general rule of transfer modes is derived.
Despite some imminent simplification this general rule may be summarized as follows.[91] The transfer of possession required by § 929 1st sentence is subject to three conditions:[92]

[89] *Baur/Stürner*, Sachenrecht[17], § 57 no. 19.
[90] This example is taken from *Baur/Stürner*, Sachenrecht[17], § 51 no. 20.
[91] Cf. *Baur/Stürner*, Sachenrecht[17], § 51 no. 19 with reference to RGZ 137, 23, 25.
[92] Cf. *Baur/Stürner*, Sachenrecht[17], § 51 no. 12.

(i) loss of possession: The transferor and all persons who may act in his place (direct possessor, possessory servant, *Geheißperson*) have to give up any form of possession.[93]

(ii) acquisition of possession: The transferee or any person who may act on his behalf (direct possessor, possessory servant, *Geheißperson*) has to obtain actual possession, *i.e.* physical control.

(iii) intention to transfer possession: The acquisition of possession by the transferee must be covered by the intention of the transferor to transfer possession, as otherwise the transferee's act would constitute unlawful interference.

The first requirement, *i.e.* loss of possession of the transferor will be met, in case the transferor himself hands over possession to the transferee as in case a direct possessor or possessory servant transfer possession according to his direction. This of course may similarly happen by handing over possession. In the alternative the former owner can instruct the direct possessor or possessory servant to conclude a new agreement on constructive possession with the new owner. If the intermediary acts accordingly the requirement of loss of possession will be met.[94] This transfer mode may not be confused with § 931, which provides for the assignment of the claim for recovery from an existing relationship of indirect possession.
Legal practice has developed a further transfer mode, the so-called *Geheißerwerb*. The transfer may also be conducted by a third party, who is not an intermediary, but acts according to the instruction of the transferor and hands over the goods to the transferee or agrees to hold possession for the latter.[95] An example would be that the finder of a thing does not hand the thing over to the original owner but directly transfers possession to a person, the thing has in the meantime been sold to.
The second requirement of a valid transfer, *i.e.* acquisition of possession, is met in case either the transferee, or an intermediary acting on his behalf, obtains possession and holds it for the transferee. In case the acquirer is able to perform physical control then a mere agreement on the transfer of possession is similarly sufficient (§ 854 subsection 2).
In parallel to loss of possession by means of a *Geheißperson* judicature and the prevailing doctrine have acknowledged the possibility of acquisition of possession by means of a *Geheißperson*. Here possession is transferred to a third party who although it does not hold possession with the intention to hold it for the possessor, still acts according to the latter's instructions (*Geheißperson* acting on behalf of

---

[93] For criticism on this dogma see *Brehm/Berger*, Sachenrecht (2000), no. 27.60.
[94] RGZ 103.151; BGH NJW 1959, 1536, 1539.
[95] BGHZ 36, 56, 60.

transferee).[96] This formation is of particular importance with regard to the chain-of-delivery (cf. *infra § 7*).
The third requirement is that the transfer of possession is covered by the intention of the transferor. The transferee must obtain possession as a consequence of the respective will of the former owner. This intention to transfer possession is not a legal act but a factual act. The only exception concerns transfer of possession by agreement under § 854 subsection 2. Here transfer of ownership consists of two agreements, one on the transfer of ownership and one as a substitute for the actual transfer on the transfer of possession. Both may coincide in a single act and by nature are legal acts.

bb) Brevi Manu Traditio

§ 929 2nd sentence provides for an alternative transfer mode commonly called *brevi manu traditio*. In case the transferor already has possession of the thing to be transferred, § 929 2nd sentence dispenses from the requirement of actual physical transfer. The general requirement that the transferor must loose any form of possession does apply unaltered. In case the transferee was the former direct possessor for the transferor this relationship of constructive possession therefore has to be terminated.
It should be noted that it is without significance from whom the transferee has obtained possession, whether he has obtained direct or indirect possession and in the latter case who holds possession for him. Further the agreement under § 929 2nd sentence may also be anticipated.
The ratio behind this 'transfer mode' is that the application of the general rule would only necessitate a subsequent retransfer.[97] In fact the principle of *traditio* in this case is curtailed by the *solo consensus* rule.[98]

cc) Constitutum Possessorium

The transfer mode of *constitutum possessorium* is available if the transferor intends to transfer ownership and at the same time retain direct possession of the asset involved. This may be of interest in case the transferor is dependent on the possibility to use the respective asset. Application of the general rule of § 929 would lead to the following result: the transferor would have to transfer possession to the transferee and subsequently conclude an (obligatory) agreement on a relationship of indirect possession, which obliges the transferee to retransfer possession to the transferor. In order to avoid this unnecessary back and forth,

---

[96] *Baur/Stürner*, Sachenrecht[17], § 51 no. 17.
[97] *Baur/Stürner*, Sachenrecht[17], § 51 no. 20.
[98] *Brehm/Berger*, Sachenrecht (2000), no. 27.38.

§ 930 provides for the *constitutum possessorium*. It is a substitute transfer mode for the acquisition of ownership under § 929 1st sentence and thus requires a real agreement in the meaning of § 929. But the actual transfer is replaced by constructive possession (*Besitzmittlungsverhältnis*): the transferor transforms his intention to hold possession as proprietary possessor into the intention to henceforth hold possession in another's interest (*i.e.* the transferee). The transferee accordingly attains the position of an indirect proprietary possessor and thus acquires ownership of the asset.

The underlying relationship of constructive possession according to § 868 may be based on usufruct, pledge, lease, tenancy and deposit or a similar relationships. Such similar relationship may arise either from contract or statute[99] (cf. *supra § 2 3. c*). Examples for further similar relationships in the meaning of § 868 arising from statute are the parental care for the children's property,[100] the relation between executer and heirs, or the relation between liquidator in bankruptcy and debtor in bankruptcy. The common feature of all relationships of constructive possession is that the possessor for another is granted a right to possession which is derived from the proprietary possessor and restricted to a limited time period. The proprietary possessor therefore must have a claim for recovery of possession against the direct possessor.

The relationship of indirect possession must be definite,[101] *i.e.* it has to spell out the rights and obligations of the parties. If the agreement on a relationship of constructive possession is void this will however not affect the transfer of ownership, as long as the owner has a right to claim recovery of possession from the direct possessor and the latter respects the proprietary possession of the owner. By contrast, the mere agreement that one will hold possession for the other without an underlying justification will not suffice.[102] This further requirement is unproblematic with respect to the examples given in § 868, but it is of some importance with regard to credit securities.

The minimum requirement for a relationship of constructive possession between the secured creditor and the party furnishing security is that the rights and duties are specified. As the concept of securities by fiduciary transfer of title have become accepted by judicature and legal doctrine, most likely the agreement that the asset is transferred as security would suffice. The rights and obligations of the

---

[99] As far as a relationship of indirect possession exists *ex lege* the mere agreement on the transfer of ownership is sufficient for a transfer under § 930, cf. *Baur/Stürner*, Sachenrecht[17], § 51 no. 24.

[100] BGH NJW 1989, 2542.

[101] *Baur/Stürner*, Sachenrecht[17], § 51 no. 22.

[102] BGH NJW 1953, 217; BGH NJW 1979, 2308; criticised by Staudinger/*Wiegand* (2004), § 930 no. 14 ff.

parties will then have to be determined according to the case law and the general usage.[103]

From the point of view of publicity the transfer mode set out in § 930 is particularly problematic in case of transfer of ownership between spouses: for example the husband by mere agreement can transfers ownership in a valuable asset to his wife, which already previously had been in co-possession of the spouses.[104]

The agreement on a relationship of constructive possession can even be concluded by means of self-contracting under § 181, *i.e.* in case the agent is authorized to dispose or by the agreement merely fulfils a pre-existing obligation vis-à-vis the principal. Constructive possession by self-contracting is of particular interest in case ownership is supposed to be transferred to a person behind the transferee, such as a commission agent who conducts a purchase for the principal in his own name. The main application of this concept therefore is an order to buy on commission.[105] It is a major interest of the principal – who will often have paid in advance – to acquire ownership as soon as possible and thus secure his property against the agent's creditors. However, the principle of publicity requires, that the agent's intention to transfer ownership is by some means made public. This can for instance be implemented by marking the respective goods with the name of the principal, or by means of storage in a separate room or warehouse. Negotiable instruments will have to be registered by an itemized list.

A prompt transfer to the principal can be reached by means of an anticipated *constitutum possessorium*: Here both the agreement on the transfer of ownership and the agreement on a relationship of constructive possession are concluded before the agent as the future direct possessor has himself obtained possession. The minimum requirement again is that the goods to be transferred and thus subject to the constructive possession are clearly determined. As soon as the agent obtains possession the principal acquires ownership after a further 'logical second' (so-called *Durchgangserwerb*). Thus the principal does not directly acquire from the contracting partner of the agent, but from the agent. During this logical second the asset belongs to the agent's property, it may be encumbered by other restricted property rights, in particular security interests.[106]

The main field of application of the transfer mode of an anticipated *constitutum possessorium* is a fiduciary transfer of title with respect to a changing stock-in-trade.[107] The party furnishing security in most cases will depend on the possibility to trade with the assets contained in the stock in order to gain the capital necessary

---

[103] *Baur/Stürner*, Sachenrecht[17], § 51 no. 22.
[104] *Baur/Stürner*, Sachenrecht[17], § 51 no. 25.
[105] *Baur/Stürner*, Sachenrecht[17], § 51 no. 30.
[106] *Baur/Stürner*, Sachenrecht[17], § 51 no. 31.
[107] *Baur/Stürner*, Sachenrecht[17], § 51 no. 31.

to repay the security holder. To this end the security holder and debtor agree that all goods, which are held in a particular room or warehouse, belong to the security holder and the security holder in addition authorizes the debtor to dispose of the goods. Now the debtor acquires ownership with delivery of the goods from a third party and on the basis of the anticipated real agreement subsequently transfers the ownership in the goods by bringing them into the respective rooms or warehouse. The security holder acquires ownership and thus may satisfy his security interest. Of course, this arrangement again falls short of the principle of publicity.[108]

The sale-and-lease-back-contract may serve as a further example for such arrangement: A is the owner of a valuable machine. In order to gain the capital for further investments he agrees with B that B shall purchase the machine and acquire ownership and subsequently lease it to A, who needs the machine for his manufacture. The lease is a relationship of constructive possession in the meaning of § 868 and § 930 respectively. The actual transfer of possession therefore is dispensable, as B would have to immediately retransfer possession to A, because the latter as the lessee is entitled to possession. This simplification of course again results in a lack of publicity.

Another example for an application of transfer by means of constructive possession is the fiduciary transfer of title: A business owner can transfer ownership in his vehicle fleet to a banking house according to § 930 as a security. As long as the agreement on the conditional ownership specifies the mutual rights and obligations this agreement is recognized as a relationship of constructive possession. It is not necessary to transfer possession in the vehicle fleet to the bank. This serves the interest of both parties: the business owner needs the vehicle fleet to run his business and the bank would otherwise have to take the vehicles in custody. The drawback of this concept is that transfer of ownership takes place without any form of publicity.

dd) Assignment of the Claim for Delivery

An owner, who is not the direct possessor of an asset, cannot transfer actual physical possession as required by § 929. He is assisted by § 931, which provides that actual transfer may be substituted by assignment of his claim for delivery against the direct possessor to the transferee. The owner can similarly transfer ownership under § 931 by assignment of a future or conditional claim for delivery.

This substitute transfer mode is of particular importance to make the sale of an asset possible, which at the time of sale is in the hand of an intermediary entitled

[108] By contrast RGZ 73, 415, 418 and RGZ 140, 223, 231 had held it to be essential that the transfer of ownership has to be perceptible for third parties.

to possession. Otherwise the owner due to the direct possessor's right to possession would not only be precluded to claim retransfer of possession immediately (*e.g.* a lessor wants to sell the asset he let to the lessee without terminating the lease contract) but would even be debarred from disposing of his asset altogether. Another advantage of this transfer mode is that it dispenses of the unnecessary transfer in case the transferee would after the transfer hand the asset over to the same direct possessor (*e.g.* the lessee).

§ 931 contains two different transfer modes, which have to be distinguished. First, the case of a transferor as indirect possessor, second the case of the transferor who does not have any possession but merely a claim for recovery of possession.

An owner who is indirect possessor may assign his claim for delivery arising from the relationship of constructive possession.[109] Such assignment is a valid transfer of indirect possession according to § 870. Provided that an agreement on transfer of ownership has been concluded the transferee acquires ownership. However, this transfer mode is excluded as far as the parties to the relationship of constructive possession have agreed that the claim may not be assigned (§ 399 2nd case).[110]

The assignment of the claim for delivery follows the general rules on assignment of rights contained in § 398 ff. An assignment can be tacitly agreed and will as a rule coincide with the agreement on the transfer of ownership. A notice to the debtor, *i.e.* the direct possessor, is not required. His legal position is not spoiled by a transfer of ownership under § 931.

The second category of cases within the scope of § 931 concerns the situation that the owner does not even hold indirect possession. As he, due to the lack of a relationship of constructive possession, cannot assign the respective claim, the claim to be assigned may be substituted by a claim arising from either unjustified enrichment (§§ 812 ff.), tort law (§ 823 ff.) or unlawful interference (§ 861). Which of these claims is precise will depend on how his loss of possession has occurred.

By contrast, the assignment of the claim for recovery arising from the right of ownership (§ 985) is a subsidiary transfer mode and may only be assigned in exceptional circumstances, *i.e.* in case the owner has no other obligatory claim for recovery. This so-called assignment of revindication (*Vindikationszession*) would be a valid transfer mode in case of things that no one holds in possession, such as a ship that has sunk or a vehicle on the moon.[111]

The restrictive approach to the assignment of the claim for revindication is a result of the concept of revindication as a inseparable part of ownership. Therefore the agreement on transfer of ownership actually would already comprise the

[109] BGH NJW 1959, 1538.
[110] Cf. BGH NJW 1979, 2037.
[111] *Avenarius*, JZ 1994, 511, 512.

assignment of the right to revindication and can accordingly not constitute a separate transfer mode. In fact, the claim for revindication is the sole remains of the power of an owner, who has lost possession. To recognise assignment of the *rei vindicatio* as substitute transfer mode, therefore, is a recognition of transfer of ownership by mere agreement and a further exemption from the principle of *traditio.*[112]

ee) Symbolic Delivery

The transfer of possession under § 929 ff. requires that the transferee obtains possession. Whether the relation of the transferee to the asset is strong enough in order to constitute possession will be determined according to §§ 854 ff. (cf. *supra § 2 4. b*). As far as the transferee by means of symbolic delivery, such as a key, obtains physical control this will of course constitute possession in the meaning of § 854 and in consequence meet the requirement of transfer of possession in the meaning of § 929. But a mere symbolic delivery that does not lead to comparable physical control, by contrast, is not recognized.[113]

ff) Title-Conferring Instruments

Title-conferring instruments are negotiable instruments in which the ownership of the respective goods is registered in such a way[114] that the transfer of possession of the goods may be substituted by the transfer of the instrument (§ 448 HGB). The transfer of the instruments conforms to the transfer mode of § 929 1st sentence. The fact that a title-conferring instrument has been issued does not preclude a regular transfer of title under § 929 1st sentence by actual transfer of the goods. Nor does it hinder the transfer mode of assignment of the claim for delivery. However, in this case the transfer mode of § 931 requires that the title-conferring instrument is also handed over to the transferee.[115]
Negotiable instruments recognized as title-conferring instruments are the negotiable warehouse receipt (§ 475g HGB), the shipping note (§ 448 in conjunction with § 444 ff. HGB) and the bill of lading (§ 647 in conjunction with 642 ff. HGB). This enumeration is exclusive, further negotiable instruments cannot attain title-conferring effect by party agreement.[116]

---

[112] *Baur/Stürner*, Sachenrecht[17], § 51 no. 38.
[113] *Joost* in MünchKomm BGB[4] VI, § 854 no. 29; Staudinger/*Wiegand* (2004), § 929 no. 65.
[114] Cf. §§ 424, 450, 650 HGB.
[115] BGHZ 49, 163; *Quack* in MünchKomm BGB[4] VI, § 931 no. 21; for details see *Schnauder*, NJW 1991, 1642 ff.
[116] *Quack* in MünchKomm BGB[4] VI, § 931 no. 21.

The legal relationship between the issuer of the instruments and the possessor is determined exclusively by the content of the negotiable instrument. Defences arising from the relationship with other former owners or transferors of the instrument are precluded.

§ 6. Double Sale of the Same Asset

As mentioned above, the sole requirement for the valid acquisition of ownership is that one of the transaction modes provided for in § 929 ff. is complied with. In general this comprises a real agreement and subsequent transfer of possession. Application of this general rule to double sale of the same asset leads to the result that the purchaser who obtains possession will also acquire ownership. This result is independent of which of the two purchasers concluded the purchase contract first. As the ownership of the transferor is not committed by the mere obligation to sell to the other (first) purchaser, the transferor at the time of transfer is still authorized. The second purchaser does not acquire from an unauthorized person, but from the owner. Double sale therefore does not fall within the scope of the rules on *bona fide*-acquisition. Good faith of the (second) purchaser accordingly is not a prerequisite for his acquisition of ownership.[117]

There is however one exception to this rule. If the second purchaser does not simply have knowledge of the prior obligation the transferor has committed himself to, but actually acquires ownership for the (sole) purpose to prevent the first purchaser from acquisition this will be regarded as a case of *mala fide* damage (cf. § 826).[118] However, this case cannot be established by merely showing that the transferee had knowledge of the prior obligation, but only by the intention to cause damage.[119] Of course, such extra-ordinary circumstances will hardly ever be corroborated.[120] But if the first purchaser can prove a case of intentional damage, then the contractual agreement between the transferor and the second purchaser are void under § 138 subsection 1. The first purchaser can claim transfer of ownership from the second purchaser, who in the meantime had acquired ownership (§ 249 in conjunction with § 826).

In case a party that has concluded a purchase contract, but has not yet acquired ownership and is afraid that the seller may have the intention to sell the goods purchased to a third party, *i.e.* to act contrary to the obligatory commitment, he may apply to the court for an interim injunction against the seller prohibiting the disposal of the goods (§ 938 subsection 2 ZPO). Such a restraining order is

---

[117] *Baur/Stürner*, Sachenrecht[17], § 5 no. 46.
[118] BGH NJW 1974, 36; BGH NJW 1981, 2184; BGH NJW 1988, 1716, 1717.
[119] Hk-BGB/*Staudinger*, § 826 no. 14.
[120] *Baur/Stürner*, Sachenrecht[17], § 5 no. 46.

comparable to an obligatory agreement not to dispose under § 135. Its effectivity against any third party therefore depends on whether the third party knows or ought to know of the prohibition.[121] This requirement fulfilled, the result is a 'division' of ownership. A disposition contrary to the restraining order transfers ownership to the third party with the exception that it is without effect as regards the protected party. Insofar the transferor remains the authorized owner. The protected party may therefore claim transfer of title from the transferor; the real agreement will be substituted by the court order. The protected party in consequence acquires ownership and can claim recovery from the second purchaser.

In case no restraining order has been applied for or such was not granted, a purchaser who did not acquire ownership, because the transferor has acted contrary to his obligation, can claim damages from the transferor. But he is not entitled to claim recovery from the other (subsequent) purchaser.

§ 7. Chain of Delivery

1. General Rule

The concept of a chain-of-delivery is not subject of separate rules of the Civil Code. The transfer of ownership therefore follows the general rules set out above (§ 929 ff.). Further sales of the same goods and direct delivery from the first seller to the last buyer will – from a legal perspective – constitute separate transactions. The real agreement always has to correspond to the respective contractual agreement (*e.g.* the goods are first transferred from A to B and subsequently from B to C). There is no possibility to directly transfer ownership from A to C.[122]

The fact that the individual contracts between the respective parties are the foundation of the chain of delivery serves legal certainty of each of the contracting parties. First, it assures that the defect of a later agreement within other limbs of the delivery chain cannot affect the validity of the former agreements. Second, the construction as individual contracts is a necessary requirement in order to enable the parties to include a reservation of title in the respective real agreement.[123]

---

[121] In case the second purchaser is *bona fide*, *i.e.* he has no knowledge of the restraining order, the rules on *bona fide*-acquisition apply (§ 135 subsection 2): the restraining order is ineffective against the third party. But of course the party applying for the restraining order may destroy the good faith of another purchaser by bringing the order to his knowledge.

[122] BGH NJW 1986, 1166; *Baur/Stürner*, Sachenrecht[17], § 51 no. 17.

[123] *Hager*, ZIP 1993. 1446, 1447.

In order not to restrict agreements which from an economic perspective avoid unnecessary cost of transaction, an exception from the general rule concerning the requirement of transfer of possession is accepted. The concept of *Geheißerwerb* is acknowledged as substitute of the *traditio* requirement.
The concept of *Geheißerwerb* conveys the idea that a third party holds physical possession of the assets involved and is willing to comply with the instructions of the respective owner. Despite the fact that the asset remains in the possession of the '*Geheißperson*' the fact that he does not hold it as proprietary possessor (cf. *supra § 2 2. c*) allows the construction of a transfer of possession from each member of the chain to the next. Although the concept of *Geheißerwerb* is generally acknowledged, the underlying dogmatic construction is again a matter of dispute.
According to the prevailing opinion, the actual transfer of possession by the direct possessor (*i.e.* the *Geheißperson*) under the direction of the transferor constitutes a *traditio* in the meaning of § 929 ff., even though the possessor does not hold possession in the name of the respective transferee (who in consequence at no point in time acquires possession), but merely follows his directions. The further transfer of possession from the first transferee and second transferor to the purchaser (that is B to C) is executed by the direct possessor who agrees to either hand over possession according to the direction of the second purchaser to the next limb of the delivery chain or follow the latter's instructions. As long as each contractual agreement is covered by a respective real agreement and the instruction to directly transfer possession to the next limb, the number of limbs of the chain of delivery is unrestricted.[124] This construction at the same time has the effect that the delivery from the first transferor to the last transferee leads to acquisition of ownership of each member of the chain.[125]
A minority opinion solves the problem of lack of actual transfer of possession by assuming that the transferor, who accepts to deliver the goods according to the directions of the transferee thereby simultaneously agrees to a relationship of constructive possession.[126] But of course this construction will hardly ever correspond to the actual intention of the concerned parties. For the '*Geheißperson*' will often be a depository or freighter and will more often than not even precisely know who at a particular moment is the owner of the involved assets.
Notwithstanding the different dogmatic constructions, all solutions lead to the result that the direct delivery from A to C leads to a prior acquisition of ownership of B. The actual transfer of possession from A to C is then ascribed to B and the transfer of possession requirement thus fulfilled.

---

[124] *Quack* in: MünchKomm BGB[4] VI, § 929 no. 146.
[125] *Quack* in: MünchKomm BGB[4] VI, § 929 no. 146; *Martinek*, AcP 188 (1988), 573, 615.
[126] *Baur/Stürner*, Sachenrecht[17], § 51 no. 17.

2. Effect of an Invalid Contract

Turning to the effect of an invalid contract in either limb of the delivery chain the *Abstraktionsprinzip* again has to be regarded. In case the contractual agreement between A and B is void this accordingly neither does affect the transfer of ownership from A to B nor from B to C. A has lost ownership and can claim compensation *ex* unjustified enrichment from B. As the transfer of ownership to C remains unaffected, and B therefore will regularly be unable to retransfer the goods to A, the latter instead will only receive compensation of the value. If the real agreement between A and B was defective and B therefore has not acquired ownership but later the goods are transferred to C, then C may acquire ownership according to the rules on *bona fide*-acquisition.

The same applies in case of a void contract between B and C. The reversal of the transaction, regularly a claim *ex* unjustified enrichment, is conducted between the parties of the respective contractual agreement. C will therefore have to retransfer the goods to B even though he has received them directly from A.

In case all contracts between the respective limbs of the chain of delivery are void the compensation *ex* unjustified enrichment will similarly follow the chain of contractual agreements. Therefore in case B cannot achieve retransfer from C, because the latter has for instance in the meantime declared insolvency, this does not free B from his obligation to compensate A. Each limb of the chain of delivery will have to bear the risk of malperformance or insolvency of his respective contracting partner.

§ 8. The Consequences of Insolvency of One of the Parties Involved

1. General Rule

The rules on the consequences of insolvency of one of the parties may be found in § 38 ff. Insolvency Act (InsO). The general rule is that all creditors of the debtor in insolvency are divided into two groups: creditors secured by means of a right *in rem* and unsecured creditors.

The first group of creditors can – depending on the underlying right *in rem* – either claim release of their property or segregation of the property from the bankrupt's estate, *i.e.* either claim recovery of their property or at least preferential payment.

By contrast the second group consists of unsecured creditors, which can only rely on an obligatory right: the remaining assets of the debtor will be subdivided between all of these unsecured creditors. They will only receive a (usually small) percentage of recovery.

It should be mentioned that the *Abstraktionsprinzip* leads to the result, that the contracting partner of the insolvent debtor will even be left with a mere claim in bankruptcy if the underlying contract is either void or has been avoided. As the defect of the obligation has no effect on the validity of the real agreement, the transfer of ownership will remain valid and accordingly the transferred goods form part of the debtors property and therefore of the bankrupt's estate. Of course the fact that the contract is void establishes a claim *ex* unjustified enrichment. However, this claim is of an obligatory nature and without protection against insolvency.
The creditor may be in a more favourable situation in case the real agreement is void, as ownership in this case reverts to the seller with retroactive effect. The owner accordingly can claim recovery of his assets. However, this only applies as far as the creditor's contractual duty was to transfer property and not to pay money. Although coins and banknotes are tangible things in the meaning of § 90 and therefore are governed by the general rules on transfer of movables, it would be a rare case that the monies received by the debtor in bankruptcy had not yet been mixed with his own monies, whereby he would acquire original ownership. In case the purchase price is settled by a bank transfer or similar means these do not even constitute tangible things. It may therefore be stated that the buyer as a general rule cannot revindicate the money even if the real agreement were void and will always be left with a percentage of recovery. Accordingly, we will only have to deal with the situation that the transferee is the debtor and ask what remedies are granted to the transferor.
The general rule may be summarized as follows: If the transferee goes bankrupt before ownership is transferred to him (without reservation), the transferor has a right *in rem* and may claim recovery. In case the transferee declares himself bankrupt after the unreserved transfer of ownership, the transferor will merely have an obligatory right. No protection is provided to him by law, neither by means of an implied reservation of title (cf. *supra § 4 4.*), nor will his situation improve in case the underlying contractual agreement is void or avoidable.

2. Possible Situations

In case one of the contracting parties declares bankruptcy the following situations have to be distinguished:

- The transferor has performed all his contractual duties and the title has passed to the debtor, while the counter-performance is still unsettled (claim in bankruptcy).
- The transferor has performed, but the real agreement is void (or has been avoided) and ownership accordingly has not passed or has reverted with retroactive effect (release from estate).

- The contracting parties have agreed to a fiduciary transfer, the creditor therefore is the legal owner. However, due to the type of security the underlying economic situation is taken into account, the debtor accordingly held to be the equitable owner (segregation of estate).
- The contractual agreement is concluded, but neither party has completely performed its obligation under the contract (choice of the insolvency administrator).

a) Claim in Bankruptcy

If the transferor has performed without any security and the title has already been transferred to the debtor without reservation, the transferor can neither claim recovery nor can he avoid the contract relying on the insolvency of the debtor. By adjudication of insolvency his obligatory claim for counter-performance is transferred into a claim in bankruptcy and will be settled according to principle of *par conditio creditorum*, *i.e.* by a percentage in bankruptcy. In case the performance the debtor was obliged to render was not payment of a sum of money, the value of the obligation will be calculated as a specific sum (§ 45 InsO) and similarly settled by a percentage in bankruptcy.[127]
This is the typical case of insolvency and covers all obligatory claims, which were established by contractual agreement with the debtor before adjudication of bankruptcy.[128] As a consequence of the abstract transfer system similarly all claims from reversed transaction due to a defect of the contractual agreement fall into this category, as well as other claims *ex* unjustified enrichment or arising from tortious acts.

b) Release from Estate

The second possible situation is that the transferor has performed, but the real agreement effecting the transfer of title is either void *ab initio* or can be avoided due to a defect, for instance duress. As the debtor in bankruptcy has not acquired ownership the goods in his possession do not belong to the estate in bankruptcy (§ 47 InsO). The transferor may revindicate his property according to § 985.
A similar situation may arise in case the transferor under a contract containing a reservation of title declares bankruptcy. Although the transferee has only acquired an equitable interest and is not yet property owner, he may – by virtue of an exception – claim release of the reserved property from the bankruptcy's estate

[127] *Ehricke* in: MünchKomm InsO, § 38 no. 59.
[128] *Ehricke* in: MünchKomm InsO, § 38 no. 59.

(§ 107 subsection 1 InsO) if he pays the purchase price still unsettled. § 107 subsection 1 InsO protects the equitable interest against insolvency.[129]
The right to claim release from the bankruptcy's estate by exception is also granted to a creditor who is not (yet) owner of the thing, because he has agreed on a fiduciary transfer of ownership to the debtor: in case the secured party declares bankruptcy the party furnishing security may claim release of the item serving as security, if it settles the instalments, even though that party is not the owner and accordingly not entitled to revindication.[130] Here again, the underlying economic situation prevails over the general rules of property law.
In case a thing, which would have been the object of a claim of release from estate, has unlawfully been disposed of by the debtor in bankruptcy before adjudication of bankruptcy (or by the insolvency administrator after that point of time), the person entitled may instead recover the consideration for repleviable goods sold by the bankrupt or trustee (substitute segregation).[131]

c) Segregation from Estate

The most important situations where a right to segregation from estate arises in the context of movable property are situations, where formal legal ownership and the actual ownership from an economic point of view differ.
In case the creditor merely has a formal position of ownership, for instance as a result of a fiduciary transfer of ownership, again the economic interest of the debtor is protected and the creditor is merely granted a right to claim segregation of the item serving as security instead of release (§ 51 InsO).[132] The same applies in case of an extended or expanded reservation of title.[133]
A similar situation may arise in case of *specificatio*: If a movable thing is conversed into a new article by a manufacturing process according to § 950, as a general rule, the manufacturer acquires original ownership. The reserved ownership of the supplier vanishes. Accordingly, the supplier would be left with an obligatory claim against the debtor and would merely receive a percentage in bankruptcy. This detrimental result can be prevented if supplier and manufacturer agree on a so-called '*Verarbeitungsklausel*' (cf. *infra § 13 3.*), that is an agreement according to which the supplier is the manufacturer in the meaning of

---

[129] *Pape/Uhlenbruck*, Insolvenzrecht, no. 648.
[130] *Bork*, Insolvenzrecht no. 240.
[131] *Bork*, Insolvenzrecht no. 244.
[132] This result, however, is criticised by *Grunsky*, JuS 1984, 497, 499, who holds that the concept of reservation of title includes that the transferor retains full ownership. Accordingly, he should be treated as such. The approach of the leading opinion instead leads to a pledge in movables without possession and therefore is a circumvention of the legislator's intention.
[133] BGH JZ 1971, 505 (extended reservation of title); BGH JZ 1971, 506 (expanded reservation of title); *Bork*, Insolvenzrecht no. 249.

§ 950 and thereby acquires ownership of the products. However, in case of insolvency of the manufacturer this 'ownership' is not fully recognised, because from an economic perspective the manufacturer has invested his resources into the products and has to be considered as the proprietor of the products, while from this matter-of-fact perspective the supplier has a position similar to a security holder. Accordingly, he is again merely granted a right to claim segregation from estate under § 51 Nr 1 InsO.[134]

The claim for segregation grants the creditor a right of preferential satisfaction.[135] In case the value of the item serving as security exceeds the unsettled debt, the remaining amount flows to the estate in bankruptcy.[136]

d) Insolvency Administrator's Choice

In case both parties to a contract have not yet completely performed at the point of time one of the parties is declared bankrupt, the insolvency administrator according to § 103 subsection 1 InsO may choose, whether or not he wants to hold on to the contract.[137] If he chooses performance he can claim performance of the other party but in turn will also have to discharge the duties of the debtor as if the latter had not been declared bankrupt. In case he refuses to do so, the transferor is left with his obligatory claim and ill thus only receive a percantage in bankruptcy (§ 103 subsection 2 InsO).[138]

The most important case, which falls within this category, is the transfer of possession under reservation of title. In case the transferee is declared bankrupt before he has settled the purchase price and the insolvency administrator either refuses to hold on to the contract or declares to do so, but does not in fact settle the debt, then the transferor may rescind the contract and claim recovery of the thing from the debtor or the liquidator according to § 985 (release from estate).[139]

The right of the insolvency administrator to choose whether or not to hold on to the contract is restricted in the insolvency of the transferor. As long as the transferee observes his duties under the contract, the insolvency administrator may not decline performance (§ 107 subsection 1 InsO). The moment the transferee settles the last instalment, ownership passes despite the insolvency of the transferor.

---

[134] *Füller* in: MünchKomm BGB[4] VI, § 950 no. 30.

[135] *Pape/Uhlenbruck*, Insolvenzrecht, no. 519.

[136] *Bork*, Insolvenzrecht no. 246.

[137] For details see *Huber*, NZI 2004, 57 ff.

[138] Cf. *Huber*, NZI 2004, 57 ff.

[139] *Pape/Uhlenbruck*, Insolvenzrecht, no. 531; *Bork*, Insolvenzrecht no. 237.

3. Specific Cases and Exceptions

A person who intends to acquire ownership through an indirect agent does not automatically acquire ownership the moment ownership is transferred to the agent. Instead the agent himself acquires ownership and will have to transfer it to the principal by a separate legal act. However, this second transfer cannot take place before a 'logical second' has passed. In case the agent is bankrupt he can no longer transfer ownership to the principal, because according to § 80 InsO his power of disposition has ceased. Both the transferor and the principal will have to enforce their rights against the agent by means of insolvency proceedings.
An exception to this rule is acknowledged in the specific situation of a contract 'for whom it may concern' (*für den, den es angeht*). That is the case where the agent wants to acquire ownership for his principal and the transferor does not care to whom he transfers property. This may in particular apply to everyday contracts where the purchase price is paid in cash. As the transferor does not merit any protection, the prevailing opinion recognizes an exception to § 164 subsection 2: the principal directly acquires ownership from the transferor.[140]

§ 9. Passing of Ownership and Passing of Risk

The German Civil Code has adopted the Roman law maxim that the burden of deterioration or loss must be born by the owner (*casum sentit dominus*) as its starting point. This rule is altered insofar as the transferor has offered delivery, but the transferee is in default of acceptance. In this case it would be inequitable to burden the transferor with the risk of accidental loss or deterioration. The same holds true in case possession has already been transferred, but ownership has not yet passed. Here the person exercising actual control must be held responsible. Due to this alterations it must be stated, that the passing of ownership and the passing of risk may in practice often coincide, but there is no rule, that this has to be so.
The relevant alterations of the – unwritten – general rule may be found in the Law of Obligations (Second Book). The basic rule is contained in § 300

> **§ 300 BGB [Creditor's Default of Acceptance]**
>
> (1) In case the creditor is in default of acceptance the debtor will only have to account for intention and gross negligence.
>
> (2) As far as the goods owed are generic goods, the risk passes at the point of time the creditor is in default of acceptance, because he does not accept the goods offered by the debtor.

[140] RGZ 100, 190, 192; *Baur/Stürner*, Sachenrecht[17], § 51 no. 43.

In addition, more specific rules are provided for in the context of the different types of contracts. The most important for the present report are the rules on sale set out in § 446 f.

> **§ 446 BGB [Passing of Risk and Liability for Charges]**
>
> The risk of accidental loss and accidental deterioration passes to the buyer when the thing sold is handed over. From that moment onwards the benefits related to the thing accrue to the buyer and charges on it are for his account. The same consequences arise if the buyer is in default in accepting delivery.
>
> **§ 447 BGB [Passing of Risk Under a Sale by Dispatch]**
>
> (1) If, at the buyer's request, the seller dispatches the thing sold to a place other than the place of performance, the risk passes to the buyer when the seller has handed the thing over to the forwarder, carrier or other person or body designated to dispatch the thing.
>
> (2) If the buyer has given specific instructions as to the method of dispatching the thing and, without urgent reason, the seller fails to comply with this instruction; the seller is liable to the buyer for damage arising from that failure.

§ 446 provides that the risk of accidental loss or deterioration of the object of sale passes to the buyer as soon as possession is transferred. According to sentence 3 the same risk also passes without actual transfer of possession in case of default of acceptance of the buyer.

During a period of default the seller is liable for any negligence. He remains liable for performance even in case of fortuitous events, unless the damage would have occurred even if performance had been made on time (§ 287).

The requirement of 'handing over' in the meaning of § 446 subsection 1 refers to transfer of physical control,[141] while the transfer of ownership may already take place as soon as the buyer obtains some other form of possession, *i.e.* possession by means of an intermediary.[142]

As the requirements for passing of risk and transfer of ownership differ, they may and often will occur the same moment, but there is no general rule to this end. This can easily be demonstrated by two examples. First, a buyer in default of acceptance is burdened by the risk of accidental loss or deterioration, but as he has not yet obtained any form of possession transfer of ownership has not yet been effected. Second, the transfer of ownership subject to a reservation of title clause

---

[141] This requirement according to § 447 will only be modified in case of express agreement of the parties.

[142] *Brehm/Berger*, Sachenrecht (2000), no. 27.21.

leads to the situation that the buyer is not yet owner, but in consequence of the transfer of possession already burdened with the risk of accidental loss or deterioration.

Part III: Original acquisition

§ 10. Original Acquisition by Accession, Confusion and Specification

1. Introduction and Concept of Original Acquisition

The Civil Code in the §§ 946 ff. acknowledges a number of different modes of original acquisition of ownership, namely attachment of a movable to an immovable or of two movables, *confusion*, *commixtio* and *specificatio*. Their common notion is that the act of acquisition is not considered to be a legal act, but instead a physical act.[143] Accordingly, the rules on legal acts contained in the General Part (First Book) are not applicable. Acquisition thus is neither dependant on the position of the original owner nor on the legal capacity of the person performing the act.

The underlying concept of all the modes of acquisition provided for in §§ 946 ff. is that goods of different owners have been mixed or confused and either cannot be separated or could only be separated with unreasonable effort. The legal order therefore in the interest of clarity and legal certainty has to decide who is to be regarded as the owner of the result of such physical act. § 946 ff. deal with the consequences of one thing becoming an inseparable part of another.[144] As far as the consequences have not otherwise been agreed upon by the parties, the loss of ownership which follows from the legal qualification of the aggregated goods as a separate object of property rights, will either be compensated by rules of property law (*i.e.* the parties of the ingredients will become co-owners) or by means of unjustified enrichment law (*i.e.* the party loosing ownership will be granted an obligatory claim for compensation).[145]

§§ 946 ff. deal with a conflict of interest between the different owners of goods, while § 950 has to decide the conflict of interest between the supplier of goods and the manufacturer, who has invested time and energy into the product. The legal order gives preference to the manufacturer, but provides for compensation of the owner of the goods. Only in case the aggregation is the result of a legal transaction, § 929 ff. will prevail over § 946.

[143] *Füller* in: MünchKomm BGB[4] VI, § 946 no. 2.
[144] *Baur/Stürner*, Sachenrecht[17], § 53 no. 1.
[145] Cf. *Wieling*, JZ 1985, 511 f.

2. The Different Types of Original Acquisition and Their Legal Consequences

a) Attachment of a Tangible Thing to an Immovable

The consequences of the connection of a movable with immovable property follow the rule *superficies solo cedit*. The owner of the real estate acquires ownership in the movable (§ 946), because a thing which is attached to immovable property looses its capacity to be the object of separate property rights. The original owner of the movable looses his property. The same applies as far as other property rights of the movable are concerned (§ 949).[146] This legal consequence is independent of who has performed the physical act and it is mandatory.[147] The intention of the legislator was to safeguard that all things, which belong to the real property from an economic perspective, are not separated by different legal consequences.[148]

Whether or not a movable has through a physical act become an essential component part of the immovable in the meaning of § 946 is to be decided in line with the legal definition contained in §§ 93 ff. It has to be stressed that the question whether or not a thing is irrevocably attached to the real property (and accordingly ownership is acquired) is not a question of fact, but a question of law. The rule will therefore even apply in case the thing could easily be separated (as the example of the washbasin demonstrates).[149] Accordingly, not only building, walls and lanterns are within the scope of § 946, but also heating installations and sanitary installations.[150]

The rule is of major importance in the context of reservation of title, because the supplier will loose his reserved ownership by original acquisition of the purchaser, if the latter attaches the goods to his real property, *i.e.* fastens the washbasin into his bathroom.

Further the application of § 946 ff. may result to a loss of restricted property rights. The rule even applies in case the owner of the real property and the owner of the movable goods are identical: as a consequence other rights *in rem* in the movable – such as pledge – are terminated.[151] There are some exceptions to this rule. For instance § 95 provides that the owner of real property does not acquire a building erected by an usufructuary or a leaseholder, if it is erected for a temporary purpose, *i.e.* for the duration of the usufruct or lease.

---

146 This prevailing opinion is criticised by *Wieling*, JZ 1985, 511, 515, who instead reintroduces the Roman law concept of *dominium dormiens*.

147 *Füller* in: MünchKomm BGB[4] VI, § 946 no. 9, 12.

148 *Füller* in: MünchKomm BGB[4] VI, § 946 no. 1.

149 *Baur/Stürner*, Sachenrecht[17], § 53 no. 6.

150 *Füller* in: MünchKomm BGB[4] VI, § 946 no. 5.

151 *Füller* in: MünchKomm BGB[4] VI, § 946 no. 2.

b) Attachment of Movables

Attachment of movables (*accessio*) arises in case different tangible things are combined in a manner that they form essential component parts of a new thing. § 947 subsection 1 provides that as a general rule the original owners of the component parts become co-owners of the new movable. The ratio of co-ownership corresponds to the proportion of the respective value of the components at the time *accessio* took place. If it is impossible to determine the ratio of value, both co-owners shall receive the same shares (cf. § 742). As far as other rights *in rem* existed in respect of the components, these rights are not terminated but instead will continue in the respective share of co-ownership.
Co-ownership once established, the relationship between the co-owners is governed by the rules of §§ 1008 ff. as well as §§ 741 ff. According to § 749 each of the co-owners can claim termination of co-ownership: the common property will then be sold and the purchase price divided between the co-owners according to their co-ownership shares.[152]
§ 947 subsection 2 alters the rules set out above in case one of the components is to be regarded as the principal part. The original owner of that principal part will acquire exclusive ownership. Other existing rights *in rem* in the principal part remain valid as rights *in rem* in the new thing, while both ownership and other rights *in rem* in the subordinate components are terminated.
According to the judicature it is a further requirement of § 947 – in contrast to § 946 – that the movables belong to different owners.[153] Legal doctrine holds the rules of *accessio* also to be applicable to different movables of one owner, but with the reservation that other restricted property rights according to sentence 2 continue with respect to the new thing.[154]
The distinction which of the both alternative rules of subsection 1 (co-ownership) and subsection 2 (exclusive ownership) applies, depends on the classification of the components either as 'essential component part' or as 'principal part'. The question whether a component is to be regarded as principal part is decided according to the common opinion, *i.e.* generally accepted standards (*Verkehrsauffassung*). It will be decisive whether the character of the thing would be considerably altered in case the other component parts were missing.[155] This, however, is independent of the value of the principal thing and the subordinate component parts.[156]

---

[152] *Füller* in: MünchKomm BGB^4 VI, § 947 no. 8.
[153] BGH NJW 1987, 774.
[154] *Füller* in: MünchKomm BGB^4 VI, § 946 no. 2 with further references.
[155] BGHZ 20, 159, 163; *Füller* in: MünchKomm BGB^4 VI, § 947 no. 5.
[156] *Füller* in: MünchKomm BGB^4 VI, § 947 no. 6.

The distinction between principal parts and subordinate parts or equal component parts poses difficulties. However, there seems to be a tendency of the judicature to either already contradict the existence of a new aggregate thing and thus preserve security rights of a supplier[157] or in the alternative at least not to classify components as principal and subordinate components, but rather establish co-ownership of the supplier.[158] This restrictive approach is further encouraged by the literal wording of § 93, according to which a thing should be categorized as an essential component part, if and only if, separation is impossible or would lead to a considerable loss in value. It may serve as an example that the engine of a motor vehicle was not considered as a constituent part of the car.[159]

As a result the categorization as principal and subordinate parts is only contemplated in extraordinary cases.[160] The judicature has for instance applied § 947 subsection 2 with respect to a machine as the principal part in the meaning of § 947 in comparison to screws, which were classified as subordinate parts.[161] Another example is the billboard, which was held to be the principal part, in comparison to a poster (subordinate part) fastened on the board.[162]

c) Intermixture of Movables

According to § 948 the rules provided for in § 947 apply *mutatis mutandis* where different corporeal things are mixed (*commixtio*) or confused (*confusio*) and the components of the different owners can either not be separated (subsection 1) or only be separated with unreasonable costs (subsection 2). The underlying rationale of the rule is to render an uneconomic procedure of separation unnecessary in the interest of the former owners.[163]

Unless one of the component parts falls within the category of principal component, the former owners acquire co-ownership. The mere fact that the component of one of the owners is larger in quantity does not qualify it as a principal component in the meaning of § 947 subsection 2.[164]

---

[157] Cf. OLG Köln NJW 1991, 2570.

[158] *Baur/Stürner*, Sachenrecht[17], § 53 no. 9; see also *Füller* in: MünchKomm BGB[4] VI, § 947 no. 6.

[159] BGHZ 18, 226, 229; BGHZ 61, 80, 81.

[160] *Baur/Stürner*, Sachenrecht[17], § 53 no. 9.

[161] BGHZ 20, 154.

[162] OLG Oldenburg NJW 1982, 1166.

[163] *Füller* in: MünchKomm BGB[4] VI, § 948 no. 1.

[164] *Baur/Stürner*, Sachenrecht[17], § 53 no. 11.

d) Processing

§ 950 on *specificatio* provides that the manufacturer of a new movable thing acquires ownership in that new thing, unless the value added by the production process is considerably lower than the value of the components used. The value relationship between the commodities used and the production is calculated by deduction of the value of the supplies from the value of the end product price.[165] In case a *specificatio* under § 950 will similarly qualify as attachment of movables according to § 950, the latter will prevail: the manufacturer therefore acquires original ownership of the products.[166]
Acquisition of ownership by the manufacturer terminates all former property rights in the supplies (*e.g.* reserved ownership of the supplier of the goods). As specification is a physical act, the consequences are independent of both the legal capacity and good faith of the manufacturer. § 950 resolves the conflict of interest between the supplier and the manufacturer to the benefit of the latter and thereby runs contrary to the general rule that the mere alteration of a substance is unable to bring about changes in property rights concerning that substance.[167] The loss of rights *in rem* of the former owner is compensated either according to a pre-existing contractual agreement or by recourse to the rules of unjustified enrichment (§ 951).
The question whether or not the product is a new thing will be decided according to the generally accepted standards, *i.e.* the common opinion (*Verkehrsauffassung*), but may be supplemented by an economic assessment.[168] The decisive factor is whether or not the nature of the goods has been altered.[169] The fact that the end product is known under another name as the supplies indicates that such a sufficient alteration has taken place.[170]
The common opinion (*Verkehrsauffassung*) will also decide whether the manufacturer has performed a *specificatio* or has merely altered the thing. For instance maintenance and repair will not be considered as *specificatio*. However, the scope of *specificatio* is widened by sentence 2: it provides that the variation of the surface by means of writing, drawing, painting, printing engraving or other similar means are presumed to be a *specificatio* in the meaning of sentence 1.

---

165 BGHZ 56, 88; BGHZ 46, 117; BGH NJW 1955, 2633. A considerable lower value of the production process is assumed in case the ratio between supplies and product is 60:100 or beyond, BGH JZ 1972, 166; BGH NJW 1995, 2633; cf. *Füller* in: MünchKomm BGB[4] VI, § 950 no. 11.
166 *Füller* in: MünchKomm BGB[4] VI, § 947 no. 11.
167 *Baur/Stürner*, Sachenrecht[17], § 53 no. 14.
168 *Füller* in: MünchKomm BGB[4] VI, § 950 no. 7.
169 *Füller* in: MünchKomm BGB[4] VI, § 950 no. 7.
170 Cf. BGHZ 56, 88; BGH NJW 1978, 697; BGH NJW 1995, 2633 with note *K. Schmidt*, JuS 1995, 1133.

As *specificatio* has far reaching consequences, the most important question in this context of course is who is to be considered as the manufacturer. Both the person actually performing the physical and the owner of the undertaking in which the manufacturing process takes place may qualify as the manufacturer in the meaning of § 950.[171] According to the judicature, the manufacturer in the meaning of § 950 is the person in whose name and interest the goods are produced.[172]
It is a matter of a long-standing dispute whether or not the rule of *specificatio* in § 950 is of a mandatory nature or leaves room for an agreement of the parties. Arguments brought forward in favour of the mandatory nature are the systematic context of the rule as well as the intention of the legislator.[173] The contrary opinion relies on the *travaux preparatoire*, which state that the possibility to agree by contract on who is supposed to be held as manufacturer in the meaning of § 950 has remained unmentioned for the mere reason that this was self-evident.[174] Further arguments for the non-mandatory nature are drawn from the context of service contracts: because the contractor rendering performance is under no duty to transfer ownership of the product (produced from supplies provided by the principal) to the principal it is assumed, that § 950 does not apply to service contracts. If this is so – according to this view – it may be inferred that a contractual agreement (such as a service contract) prevails over the general rules on original acquisition of ownership.[175]
Despite these arguments the prevailing opinion holds on to the mandatory nature of § 950.[176] Yet, it recognises other solutions which grant more flexibility. First, an agreement by which the parties do not alter the legal consequences of § 950, but instead agree who is supposed to be deemed the manufacturer in the meaning of § 950 is accepted.[177] Second, the possibility that supplier and manufacturer can conclude an anticipated *constitutum possessorium* and thereby (re-)transfer ownership to the supplier is stressed. The judicature also holds on to the mandatory nature, but evenly permits the contractual modification of the rule who is deemed manufacturer of the products.[178]
In legal practice agreement of a so-called processing clause (*Verarbeitungs-klausel*) between the conditional vendor and the conditional purchaser is

---

[171] *Füller* in: MünchKomm BGB[4] VI, § 950 no. 16.
[172] BGHZ 112, 243, 249 ff.; BGHZ 20, 159, 163; BGHZ 14, 114, 117.
[173] *Füller* in: MünchKomm BGB[4] VI, § 950 no. 14 ff.; *Medicus*, Bürgerliches Recht, no. 519.; *Wadle*, JuS 1982, 477, 479.
[174] *Baur/Stürner*, Sachenrecht[17], § 53 no. 15; of contrary opinion *Wadle*, JuS 1982, 477; both with reference to Protokolle III 239, 242 ff.
[175] *Baur/Stürner*, Sachenrecht[17], § 53 no. 15; *Flume*, NJW 1950, 841, 843 ff.; of other opinion *Wadle*, JuS 1982, 477, 479.
[176] *Füller* in: MünchKomm BGB[4] VI, § 950 no. 15 (with further references).
[177] *Füller* in: MünchKomm BGB[4] VI, § 950 no. 18 ff.
[178] Cf. BGHZ 14, 114, 117; BGHZ 20, 159.

acknowledged, according to which the conditional vendor, who has reserved ownership, is deemed to be the manufacturer in the meaning of § 950.[179] By means of this processing clause the manufacturer assumes the duty to produce for the supplier of the goods, regularly the conditional vendor.[180] However, the legal consequence of such a clause is also a matter of dispute. The judicature relies upon a wide concept of manufacturer, while part of legal doctrine points to the contractual agreement. Both views lead to an original acquisition of ownership by the supplier. A deviating opinion argues that the question, who is held to be the supplier under § 950 has to be decided on the basis of objective criteria,[181] therefore the processing clause is held to contain nothing else but an anticipated *constitutum possessorium.*[182]

These different opinions lead to a considerable difference in result, as the construction as *constitutum possessorium* implies, that the manufacturer acquires ownership and then, that is after the famous 'logical second', transfers ownership to the supplier.[183] The fact that the manufacturer is owner for a logical second is called '*Durchgangserwerb*'. This construction is criticized because it gives preference to other creditors of the manufacturer over the interest of the supplier, which consequence is a major argument in favour of the admissibility of the processing clauses and their construction leading to direct original acquisition of the supplier.[184]

3. The Legal Consequences

In case an owner of a component part or supplies looses his ownership this at the same time terminates all other existing property rights in the movable (§ 949 and § 950 subsection 2 respectively).[185] The new owner acquires unburdened property. In case the previous owners become co-owners of the common property, the law provides for a substitution by operation of law: other property rights continue in the respective co-ownership shares.

The status of ownership effected by § 946 ff. is final. Therefore even in case of later separation of the components ownership rests with the person who has

---

[179] BGHZ 20, 159, 162; BGHZ 46, 117, 118 ff.; BGH NJW 1991, 1480, 1481; Hk-BGB/*Eckert* § 950 no. 8.

[180] *Füller* in: MünchKomm BGB[4] VI, § 950 no. 24.

[181] *Westermann*/Gursky § 53 III 2 d; *Wadle*, JuS 1982, 477, 481.

[182] Palandt/*Bassenge* BGB[64] § 950 no. 13; *Ehricke* in: MünchKomm InsO, § 47 no. 108; Staudinger/*Wiegand* (2004), § 950 no. 41.

[183] *Westermann*/Gursky § 53 III 2 d; *Medicus*, Bürgerliches Recht no. 515 ff., 519.

[184] *Füller* in: MünchKomm BGB[4] VI, § 950 no. 25; Hk-BGB/*Eckert* § 950 no. 8.

[185] *Füller* in: MünchKomm BGB[4] VI, § 949 no. 1 ff.

acquired it under § 946 ff. and does not revert to the previous owners of the respective component parts or goods.[186]

The previous owner who lost his property as a consequence of § 946 ff. or § 950 is granted a claim for compensation against the new owner (§ 951). § 951 on the compensation of the previous owner refers to the rules of unjustified enrichment law. The amount of compensation will be estimated according to the current market price (§ 818 subsection 2).[187] The general rule is, that the previous owner is compensated by an amount of money but may not reclaim his property (*i.e.* restitution in kind).[188] Compensation according to § 951 only takes place with respect to the previous owner and the person who has acquired ownership. By contrast all other property rights that have been terminated by the original acquisition remain without compensation.

Of course such a claim for compensation *ex* unjustified enrichment is no full replacement for the ownership lost. This is in particular true in case the new owner declares bankruptcy: Then the claim for release from estate is substituted by a mere percentage in bankruptcy. This of course is one of the most persuasive reasons why the judicature tries to construe the provisions on original acquisition narrowly and thereby prevent the termination of ownership in the first place, or at least prefers the finding of co-ownership over the result of exclusive ownership of one party.[189]

§ 11. *Bona Fide*-Acquisition

1. General Concept

The rules on good faith acquisition in movables may be found directly following the rules on transfer of title in movable property (§§ 932 - 936). Their structure also relies on the rules on transfer of title in §§ 929 - 931: each separate rule on good faith acquisition mirrors one of the rules on transfer of title from an authorized person. Additional specific rules on *bona fide*-acquisition concern registered ships (§ 932a) as well as acquisition of property in the course of a commercial transaction § 366 HGB. The rules provided for by law are enumerate.[190]

---

186 *Füller* in: MünchKomm BGB^4 VI, § 946 no. 10, § 947 no. 9.

187 BGHZ 5, 197, 201 f.; BGHZ 17, 236, 239 f.; *Füller* in: MünchKomm BGB^4 VI, § 951 no. 24.

188 § 951 subsection 2 provides for an exception. In case the former owner is unable to obtain compensation he may under particular circumstances take recourse to means of self-help and withdraw the goods.

189 *Baur/Stürner*, Sachenrecht^{17}, § 53 no. 23.

190 On the extension to good faith acquisition of equitable interests cf. *infra 2*.

According to general rules a disposition of movables will only be valid in case it is performed by a person authorized[191] or that person has later ratified the disposition (§ 185). As the acquirer of goods usually has no possibility to inquire into the authority of the transferor, the imposition of this general rule on the rules on transfer and the according transferee's burden to examine the transferor's authority would therefore impede the fluency and ease of legal transactions.[192] Accordingly the law under certain circumstances provides for a good faith acquisition and protects the *bona fide* partner and his faith in the validity of the agreement.[193] This general interest in the ease of legal transactions is granted preference over the interest of the owner to retain his legal position. In case the further requirements are satisfied, the transferor will acquire property free of any encumbrances. The owner will loose his property and will have to turn to the transferor for compensation and damages.
The rules on good faith acquisition from an unauthorized person are founded on two general principles: first that the owner has – in a wide sense – contributed to the appearance of a right or legal position of the unauthorized transferor. This aspect is usually referred to as *Veranlassungsprinzip.* Second, on a balance of interest between the person who may loose its legal position (ownership or other property rights) and the *bona fide* transferee, the notion of protection of legal transactions (*Vertrauensschutz* or *Verkehrsschutz*).[194]
The underlying conflict of interest is solved by means of a rule, according to which a *bona fide*-acquisition from an unauthorized person is only possible as far as the person owning property rights is responsible for the *prima facie* appearance of the transferor as the owner. The owner must himself be responsible for the transfer of possession. *Bona fide*-acquisition therefore requires, that the owner has deliberately[195] disposed of the possession of the thing (*Veranlassungsprinzip*).[196] The ratio behind this rule is that the owner can and should examine the trustworthiness and reliability of any person he entrusts his possessions to.[197] Further he has the possibility to reduce the risk that an intermediary later on disposes of his belonging without authority and thereby enables a *bona fide*-acquisition, by taking precautions to destroy the good faith of any prospective transferee. For example the creditor who accepts a fiduciary transfer in a car as security can ask the debtor furnishing security to hand over the registration

---

[191] This is at the same time an unmentioned requirement of § 929 ff.
[192] *Baur/Stürner*, Sachenrecht[17], § 1 no. 12.
[193] *Quack* in: MünchKomm BGB[4] VI, § 932 no. 1.
[194] Cf. *Quack* in: MünchKomm BGB[4] VI, § 932 no. 3 ff.
[195] On the exception concerning money and bearer securities (§ 935 subsection 2) cf. *infra 8*.
[196] This rule is criticised by *Thorn*, ZEuP 1997, 442, 473 ff., because it is not apparent for third parties whether or not this requirement is met.
[197] *Quack* in: MünchKomm BGB[4] VI, § 932 no. 2.

certificate. This is a very effective measures of protection, as a person who buys a car, but does not receive the registration certificate from the transferor, will – leaving exceptional circumstances aside – not be held to be *bona fide*.[198] Similarly a library can stamp its books and accordingly prevent the good faith of any transferee.

This means of protection already point towards the second crucial requirement of *bona fide*-acquisition: the transferee has to *bona fide* believe in the ownership of the transferor and this good faith has to be founded on the legitimizing appearance of the transferor's legal position. Such legitimizing appearance can be justified by either the transferor's direct possession or his power to transfer possession to the transferee respectively (*Vertrauensprinzip*).[199]

It should be mentioned that there is a tendency of the judicature to impose more strict requirements with regard to the transferee's good faith and to establish duties of enquiry into and examination of the authority of the transferor. This of course in effect leads to a reduction of the scope of application of *bona fide*-acquisition in favour of the interest of the owner to protect his legal position.[200]

2. Scope of Application

The rules on good faith acquisition always apply if the transfer of title would be valid according to the rules of § 929 ff. but for the lack of the transferor's authority.[201] The reason why the transferor does not have authority to transfer ownership is without significance. Accordingly, the rules apply to all cases in which the transferor originally was the owner of the thing transferred, but in the meantime has disposed of his ownership otherwise (*e.g.* double sale), has lost his legal position as owner for other reasons (*e.g.* original acquisition of a third party). But it also covers the situation that the transferor never was the proprietor of the thing he transfers (*e.g.* the transferor was merely an intermediary of the former owner). The only prerequisite is that the transferor lacks authority the moment the transfer takes place.

There is a separate specific rule for the situation that the transferor did have authority at the time the transfer took place, but lost this legal position, because the legal transaction that led to his authority was avoidable. In case the avoidance is successful the transferor looses his ownership with retroactive effect. The acquisition of ownership of a third party transferee will accordingly be defective because of the lack of authority of the transferor. The rules on *bona fide*-acquisition in general apply, but with the reservation that in case the transferee

---

198 Cf. BGH NJW 1991, 1416.

199 BGHZ 10, 81.

200 Kritisch *Quack* in: MünchKomm BGB^4 VI, § 932 no. 1.

201 *Quack* in: MünchKomm BGB^4 VI, § 932 no. 6.

knows, or owing to gross negligence does not know, that the prior transaction to the transferor is avoidable, this will exclude the possibility of *bona fide*-acquisition (§ 142 subsection 2).[202]

Above we have seen that the situation of double sale is not solved by recourse to the rules on *bona fide*-acquisition, because the mere fact that a thing has been sold to two different persons does in itself not have any effect on the property rights in the asset. The transferor has committed himself to two duties, which he thus cannot possibly both fulfil. Which of the two buyers will acquire ownership will depend solely on whom the transferor transfers ownership to. However, in particular circumstances the second purchaser may obtain ownership by means of a *bona fide*-acquisition: This may occur in case the transferor has already transferred ownership to the first purchaser but still holds possession of the thing (for instance because he promises to keep the goods in safe custody for the first purchaser until the latter comes to collect them). If he now transfers ownership to the second purchaser the latter may acquire ownership according to the rules on *bona fide*-acquisition (§ 932 ff.). In case the further requirements of a valid transfer, in particular transfer of possession, are met, he will acquire ownership. The first purchaser looses his and will have to turn to the transferor for compensation.

The rules on *bona fide*-acquisition do not apply in case of insolvency of the owner. According to § 81 subsection 1 sentence 2 InsO the owner after declaration of insolvency lacks the authority to transfer ownership. Similarly the absolute lack of authority to dispose according to §§ 1365, 1369 (disposal of the entire property of one spouse or disposition of household items) prevails over the rules on *bona fide*-acquisition.[203]

The categorization of goods, which can be acquired by *bona fide*-acquisition, resembles the scope of application of goods that fall under the transfer of movables according to § 929 ff., *i.e.* movable property in the meaning of § 90 (cf. *supra § 1 a*). The rules therefore also apply with respect to negotiable instruments, money, and bearer securities, as to works of art[204]. In parallel to the extension of the rules on transfer of movables from an authorized person, so are the rules on transfer from an unauthorized person extended to acquisition of equitable interests. Thus an equitable interest arising from a sale subject to a reservation-of-title clause may be acquired under the rules on *bona fide*-acquisition of movables, but subject to the further requirement, that the position of the *bona fide* transferee

---

[202] BGH NJW-RR 1987, 1456, 1457.

[203] Cf. *Wolf*, JZ 1997, 1087 ff.

[204] But see the Directive 93/7/EEC on the reatransfer of pieces of national art which have been transferred to foreign countries, OJ March 27th, 1993, no. L 74, 74 and the respective acts transforming the directive into German law: Kulturgutsicherungsgesetz and Kulturgüterrückgabegesetz, October 15th 1998, BGBl I 3162.

will depend on the existence of the sales contract. The concept of *bona fide*-acquisition can merely replace the authority of the transferor. Consequently the good faith cannot replace the lack of existence of the equitable interest itself. A *bona fide*-acquisition of a non-existent equitable interest therefore is impossible.[205]

3. Restriction of *Bona Fide*-Acquisition to 'Trade Transactions'

As a general rule *bona fide*-acquisition is possible with respect to all forms of transaction. No distinction is drawn between gratuitous acquisition and acquisition for consideration.[206] Again the validity of the transfer is completely independent of the underlying contractual or other obligation to transfer. Accordingly, a person who receives property as a present from an unauthorized person may equally acquire ownership *bona fide*. However, the fact that he has gratuitously received the property of another does lead to consequences with respect to the rules on unjustified enrichment. The rules discriminating against gratuitous *bona fide*-acquisition from an unauthorized person therefore are not provided for in the context of transfer of title, but are comprised in the rules on the compensation for unjustified enrichment.[207]

Generally a *bona fide*-acquisition includes a valid legal basis for the right to retain property of the thing. Accordingly, the rules on unjustified enrichment are excluded insofar as the relationship between the former owner and the *bona fide* transferee is concerned. Of course the transferor, who has performed the transfer without authority, will be held responsible. He is under a duty to restore the benefits received from the third party in return for the unauthorized transfer (§ 816 sentence 1). This rule is modified in case the third party has acquired ownership without consideration: the duty to return the benefits received extends to the transferee. He has to return what he has received by means of the unauthorized transaction, *i.e.* he regularly is under a duty to retransfer ownership to the former owner. In case he is no longer able to retransfer ownership he is under a duty to compensate for its value (§ 818 subsection 2).

The combined rules of the abstract transfer system and on *bona fide*-acquisition would lead to the consequence, that the owner may loose ownership also in cases where the legal order regards the outcome to be unjustified and is compensated only with an obligatory claim for retransfer of compensation of value. This necessitates a further restriction of the application of the rules on *bona fide*-acquisition: *bona fide*-acquisition is only acceptable insofar as there is an actual

---

205 *Baur/Stürner*, Sachenrecht[17], § 59 no. 40.

206 *Quack* in: MünchKomm BGB[4] VI, § 932 no. 7.

207 *Karner*, ZfRV 2004, 83, 86, even asserts that the result of property law is corrected by means of unjustified enrichment law.

change of legal position, not merely a formal change. This requirement is referred to as the requirement that the legal transaction constitutes a 'trade transaction' (*Verkehrsgeschäft*), but this term is misleading, as far as it may be misunderstood as a requirement of commercial context. A trade transaction describes the situation of a transfer based on a legal transaction whose transferor and transferee are not identical, neither from a legal nor a factual perspective.[208] This further requirement does not only exclude *bona fide*-acquisition of title *ex lege* and original acquisition, but also such transactions where there is no real change of the person entitled,[209] *i.e.* the transfer only has technical character.[210] This for instance would be the case if A, the managing party of company B, sells 'his car' – which in fact is still the conditional property of the seller – to B in order to use it as his company car. The underlying notion is that *bona fide*-acquisition is intended to serve the efficiency of legal transactions and therefore must be excluded in case there is no real legal transaction that assumes protection.

There is a further particularly problematic situation, which is a matter of dispute. Should the retransfer from the transferee to the unauthorized transferor transfer ownership to the latter with the result that the unauthorized person acquires full ownership and in relation to the former owner is merely under an obligatory duty to retransfer ownership[211] or should ownership automatically revert to the former owner? In order to give a comprehensive answer the following types of cases have to be distinguished:

The first category covers the so-called 'initially intended retransfer' (*anfänglich beabsichtigter Rückerwerb*).[212] Here the unauthorized transferor already at the time of the transfer to the *bona fide* transferee plans to later acquire ownership from that *bona fide* transferee. According to the prevailing opinion he cannot acquire ownership by means of such retransfer. Instead ownership reverts to the former owner.

The same applies in case the transfer from the unauthorized person to the transferee lacks a legal basis, for instance because the underlying contractual agreement is invalid. As the retransfer of ownership as an obligation *ex* unjustified enrichment it does not qualify as a trade transaction.[213] The unauthorized transferor does not acquire ownership but again the ownership will instead revert to the former owner.[214]

---

208 *Quack* in: MünchKomm BGB[4] VI, § 932 no. 18.

209 *Baur/Stürner*, Sachenrecht[17], § 52 no. 5.

210 *Brehm/Berger*, Sachenrecht (2000), no. 27.86.

211 Hk-BGB/*Eckert*, § 932 no. 2.

212 *Baur/Stürner*, Sachenrecht[17], § 52 no. 34.

213 *Zeranski*, JuS 2002, 340, 341.

214 See on the prevailing opinion *Baur/Stürner*, Sachenrecht[17], § 52 no. 2; *Schwab/Prütting*, Sachenrecht[31], no. 438; of other opinion Palandt/*Bassenge* BGB[64], § 932 no. 17; *Quack* in: MünchKomm BGB[4] VI, § 932 no. 61.

This principle, that the unauthorized transferor should not be able to acquire ownership by means of a merely transitional acquisition by a *bona fide* third party, will also be applied in case the transaction is not intended to actually confer ownership to the third party unconditionally. The transfer of a security interest by means of fiduciary transfer may serve as example. As soon as the transferor repays the loan he has secured by the transfer as a consequence the ownership of the third party is terminated by fulfilment of the condition precedent and ownership would usually fall back to the transferor. If the transferor lacked authority it instead will revert to the original owner.
If none of these three categories mentioned applies then the transferor may acquire full ownership by means of retransfer from a *bona fide*-transferee.

4. The 'Legitimizing Appearance of Possession'

The concept of *bona fide*-acquisition relies on the good faith of the transferee which is based on the legitimate expectation that the transferor's possession of the respective asset at the same time is an indication of his ownership. If the transferee relies on this legitimizing appearance (*Rechtsscheintatbestand*) he is worthy of protection. Therefore the nature of possession of the transferor must be of a kind that the transferee's reliance in the possession of the transferor appears to be reasonable and the transferee in his reliance is worth of such protection.[215]
This requirement varies according to the different modes of *bona fide*-acquisition. It is met, if one of the following situations applies: the transferor hands over the thing to the transferee (§ 932 subsection 1 sentence 1), the transferee had already at some earlier point in time received the thing from the transferor (§ 932 subsection 1 sentence 2) or the transferor transfers indirect possession to the transferee (§ 934 1st case). Under § 933 the transferee may obtain ownership if and only if he (later) obtains possession of the thing from the transferor and at that moment is still in good faith.
The above mentioned rules on *bona fide*-acquisition seem to indicate a further requirement, namely that the transferor originally had possession and later transferred it to the transferee. Despite this common notion, no general principle that *bona fide*-acquisition always requires prior possession of the transferor may be derived from these rules.[216] Under § 934 2nd case the essential requirement is not that the transferor had prior possession, but merely that the transferee at some point obtains possession. Accordingly, a legitimate expectation of the transferee that the transferor is the owner of the thing may not only rely on the transferor's

---

215 *Baur/Stürner*, Sachenrecht[17], § 52 no. 3.
216 *Quack* in: MünchKomm BGB[4] VI, § 932 no. 16.

actual possession but also on the ability of the transferor to arrange the transfer of possession to the transferee (so-called *Besitzverschaffungsmacht*).
As far as possession of the transferor is required under some rules, both direct and indirect possession will suffice. Both an indirect possessor and a possessory servant can therefore also perform the actual transfer.
Whether this rule may be extended to also cover a person, who acts for the unauthorized transferor, but does not exercise possession for that transferor (that person is usually called a '*Geheißperson*') is a matter of dispute. Even in case the *Geheißperson* does on instruction of the transferor transfer possession to the transferee, the requirement that the possession has to be transferred *from* the transferor to the transferee is still lacking. However, in case the *Geheißperson* does act in accordance with the direction of the transferor and hands over the thing to the transferee, who trusted that the transferor was at the same time the legitimate owner, then this form of tradition is also held to be sufficient.[217]
The underlying reason why the *Geheißperson* transfers possession to the transferee is held to be irrelevant. The Federal Supreme Court has approved of a *bona fide*-acquisition under § 932 subsection 1 in a case where the unauthorized transferor has sold a thing of a third party and that third party (*i.e.* the owner) subsequently transferred possession directly to the purchaser, believing that the transferor had concluded the contract under her name.[218] According to the reasoning of the court the owner was a supposed *Geheißperson* of the unauthorized transferor and has effected the transfer of possession in the transferor's name. Thus the transfer requirement under § 932 subsection 1 sentence 1 was met, because the question whether or not the owner is held to be a *Geheißperson* has to be judged from the point of view of the transferee.[219]
In legal doctrine it has time and again been criticized that possession alone does no longer confer the legitimate expectation that the possessor also be the owner, because possession as means of publicity has lost its significance (cf. *supra § 2 3. b*).[220] However, the prevailing opinion points out that first, no alternative basis for legitimate reliance is available, and second, that there may lie some truth

---

[217] BGHZ 36, 56, 60 with note *von Caemmerer*, JZ 1963, 586 ff.; BGH NJW 1979, 203; BGH NJW 1973, 141; *Baur/Stürner*, Sachenrecht[17], § 52 no. 13; *Brehm/Berger*, Sachenrecht (2000), no. 27.55; *Quack* in: MünchKomm BGB[4] VI, § 932 no. 17.

[218] BGHZ 36, 56, 60 with critical note by *von Caemmerer*, JZ 1963, 586 ff.; BGH NJW 1974, 1132, 1134; criticised by *Zeranski*, JuS 2004, 340, 345.

[219] BGH NJW 1974, 1132, 1133. This decision, however, has been frequently criticised, see *Baur/Stürner*, Sachenrecht[17], § 52 no. 13; *Brehm/Berger*, Sachenrecht (2000), no. 27.56; *Martinek*, AcP 188 (1988), 573, 627; *Picker*, NJW 1974, 1790 ff., but has also met with approval: Staudinger/*Wiegand* (2004), § 932 no. 24; Westermann/*Gursky* I § 47 I 1 a. Also compare BGH ZIP 1993, 98.

[220] *Rebe*, AcP 173 (1973), 186, 193 ff. with further references; cf. *Kindl*, AcP 201 (2001), 391, 393.

in the criticism but it is not of the same force in respect of the ability to direct a third person to transfer possession (*Besitzverschaffungsmacht*).[221]

5. The Requirement of Transfer of Physical Control and its Modifications

As mentioned above the possibility of a *bona fide*-acquisition is not *per se* restricted in case the transferor not even holds possession of the thing. The basis for the legitimate expectation of the transferee therefore is not only possession itself, but also the ability to direct another to transfer possession. The *Besitzverschaffungsmacht* will regularly arise from the fact that the transferor has (indirect) possession, but may also lie in the 'assignment' of a non-existent claim for recovery or the ability to instruct a *Geheißperson* to transfer possession. From these rules another requirement can be derived: the sole fact that the transferor's possession generates a legitimate expectation of the transferee on its own can never be sufficient, unless the transferee in consequence does actually obtain possession.

The only general rule derived from all modes is that the transferee will only acquire ownership in case the transferor does not retain any kind of possession after the transfer, not even indirect possession.[222] By contrast the question, what requirements the transferor's possession must meet prior to the transfer, cannot be answered in common for all the provisions on *bona fide*-acquisition, but has to be discussed separately for each of the different modes of acquisition.

a) Brevi Manu Traditio

The *traditio* requirement for a *bona fide*-acquisition under § 932 subsection 1 2nd sentence is met if the transferee obtains possession of the thing either directly from the transferor or from another person, who acts in accordance with the directions of the transferor, *i.e.* from a *Geheißperson*.[223] This requirement for instance is met in case the former direct possessor and assumed owner of the thing has transferred possession to the person who – authorized by the former possessor (the assumed owner) – now transfers possession to the transferee.[224]

In comparison to the mode of acquisition from an authorized person under § 929 sentence 2 the additional requirement of § 932 subsection 1 sentence 2 therefore is, that the transferee obtains possession *from the transferor*, while under § 929 the transferee may obtain possession from any other person. This further

---

[221] *Quack* in: MünchKomm BGB[4] VI, § 932 no. 16; see on the requirement of complete loss of possession under § 929 *supra § 5 4*.

[222] BGHZ 56, 123, 129 f.

[223] *Quack* in: MünchKomm BGB[4] VI, § 932 no. 56.

[224] Cf. *Baur/Stürner*, Sachenrecht[17], § 52 no. 16.

requirement is essential to establish a basis for the legitimate expectation that the transferee believes the transferor to be the owner.[225] The transferee not only has to obtain possession, but most importantly the transferor must loose any form of possession.[226]

b) Constitutum Possessorium

The mere transfer of ownership by an unauthorized person by means of a real agreement and a *constitutum possessorium* is no sufficient basis for *bona fide*-acquisition.[227] The transferee will only acquire ownership in case the thing (later) is actually handed over to him and he at that time is still in good faith. Transfer of possession in this case means that the transferee obtains exclusive possession.[228] This, however, does not exclude that intermediaries act in place of the transferee.[229]
This mode of *bona fide*-acquisition is a good example for the rule set out above, that the mere prior possession of the transferor is not regarded as a sufficient basis for the legitimate expectation of the transferee that the transferor also is the owner. Instead the legal prerequisite also includes the solid manifestation of possession of the transferee, that is exclusive possession of the acquirer or his intermediaries and complete dispossession of the transferor.[230] Although § 933 is modelled after the rule in § 930 it is in fact not a modification of that rule, but rather an exclusion of *bona fide*-acquisition by means of a *constitutum possessorium*, because on close examination § 933 requires an anticipated real agreement and a subsequent actual transfer of possession. Leaving aside that agreement and transfer do not take place simultaneously, these requirement exactly resemble those of § 929 sentence 1 instead of § 930.[231] The additional requirement of actual (subsequent) transfer of possession is of some importance in practice, as this effectively rules out the *bona fide*-acquisition of a credit security by means of fiduciary transfer: in general the transfer of security interest will fail due to lack of actual transfer of possession.

---

[225] *Zeranski*, JuS 2004, 340, 346.
[226] Cf. BGHZ 56, 123, 129 f.
[227] *Quack* in: MünchKomm BGB[4] VI, § 933 no. 1.
[228] Cf. BGHZ 67, 207, according to which unilateral removal is insufficient, even in case the transferee was authorized to take the goods away. See on this subject *Musielak*, JuS 1992, 713, 718.
[229] A mere symbolic transfer is not sufficient: OLG München NJW 1970, 667 (short test drive); OLG Frankfurt BB 1976, 573 (attachment of a sign).
[230] *Baur/Stürner*, Sachenrecht[17], § 52 no. 17.
[231] Staudinger/*Wiegand* (2004), § 933 no. 6; *Baur/Stürner*, Sachenrecht[17], § 52 no. 17.

Due to the exclusion of *bona fide*-acquisition by *constitutum possessorium* described above, there is a substantial risk for a creditor who asks a fiduciary transfer that he will not acquire any security interest in case the debtor is not owner of the goods transferred. Thus there has been the attempt to design the grant of a security in a mode falling within the scope of § 934 1st alternative and thereby circumventing the stricter rule of § 933.

The following may serve as an example:[232] if the debtor transfers title in his stock of goods to his bank as a security and agrees on a *constitutum possessorium* and the debtor therefore keeps direct possession of the stock, then the creditor will only acquire the security interest in case the debtor actually was the owner of the goods (§ 930) or the creditor later on actually takes possession of the goods (§ 933), which of course hardly ever will be the case. If the debtor by contrast transfers possession to a warehouse and accordingly has a claim for surrender from this legal relationship (usually a contract of bailment), then the debtor and creditor can provide for a security by real agreement and the assignment of the claim for delivery against the bailor. In case the debtor does lack title, the creditor may *bona fide*-acquire ownership under § 934 1st alternative.

However, whether this attempt to circumvent the rules of § 933 by a capricious manipulation will be crowned by success is rather doubtful, in particular if this construction is already predetermined by the standard terms of contract. Here the *bona fide*-acquisition will most likely fail for lack of good faith. The creditor will be confronted with the assertion that he himself obviously was not quite convinced that the debtor actually was the legitimate owner of the stocks transferred, and even though perhaps not *mala fide*, at least was grossly negligent.[233]

c) Assignment of the Claim for Recovery

§ 934 actually provides for two different alternatives of *bona fide*-acquisition, the requirements of transfer of possession therefore have to be examined separately:

The first alternative applies where the transferor is in fact the indirect possessor of the thing he intends to transfer and assigns the existent[234] claim for recovery of possession arising from the relationship of constructive possession to the transferee. The transferee can thereby acquire ownership even though he does not obtain direct possession of the thing transferred (§ 934 1st alternative). This exception from the general rule, that the transferee has to obtain direct possession

---

232 The example is taken from *Brehm/Berger*, Sachenrecht (2000), no. 27.65.

233 *Quack* in: MünchKomm BGB^4 VI, § 033 no. 19, § 934 no. 19.

234 *Baur/Stürner*, Sachenrecht^{17}, § 52 no. 21.

is often criticised as a inconsistency between the rules of § 933 and § 934.[235] However, the Federal Supreme Court has ruled that this inconsistency has to be accepted as the will of the legislator.[236] Another part of legal doctrine disagrees: according to this opinion § 933 and § 934 1st alternative are not inconsistent, because the main prerequisite of *bona fide*-acquisition is not that the transferee obtains possession, but rather that the unauthorized transferor gives up any kind of physical control of the thing transferred. The justified distinction between § 933 and § 934 1st alternative accordingly is to be seen in the fact that in case of § 933 the transferor is the intermediary and therefore does not give up physical control, while in the case of § 934 the intermediary is a third party. Accordingly only § 934 satisfies the requirement that the transferor looses any kind of physical control.[237]

Another dispute concerns the question whether or not *bona fide*-acquisition by assignment of the claim for recovery of possession is valid in case the intermediary does indirectly possess for the transferee, but at the same time also possesses with the intention to possess in the name of the former owner. Accordingly, the transferee only acquires secondary possession instead of exclusive indirect possession (so-called *Nebenbesitz*). However, the judicature of the *Reichsgericht* did not accept the concept of secondary possession and ruled that the fact that the intermediary agrees to hold possession for the transferee automatically terminates the indirect possession of the former owner.[238] The prevailing legal doctrine disagrees, because the transferee only obtains secondary possession and this position is not held to be sufficient physical control to satisfy the requirements of *bona fide*-acquisition under § 934 1st alternative.[239]

§ 934 2nd alternative applies in the situation that the transferor does not even have indirect possession and accordingly also lacks a claim for recovery of possession. The assignment of a non-existent claim for recovery of possession does not suffice to justify *bona fide*-acquisition, which will therefore only be granted in

---

235 *Kindl*, AcP 201 (2001), 391, 397 ff. with further references; *Picker*, AcP 188 (1988), 511, 515 ff.

236 BGHZ 50, 45, 51 f.

237 BGH NJW 1959, 1536; BGHZ 50, 45, 52; *Baur/Stürner*, Sachenrecht[17], § 52 no. 20 with fn. 4; cf.; critical *Kindl*, AcP 201 (2001), 391, who draws attention to the fact that the requirement of complete loss of possession is only relevant insofar as the transferor has formerly had possession at all; see also *Picker*, AcP 188 (1988), 511, 518.

238 RGZ 135, 75; RGZ 138, 265. Similarly BGH NJW 1979, 2037. See for agreement *Zeranski*, JuS 2004, 340, 343.

239 *Baur/Stürner*, Sachenrecht[17], § 52 no. 24; similarly in result *Kindl*, AcP 201 (2001), 391, 408 ff.; see on this point further *Tiedtke*, WM 1979, 1142, 1143 f.; *Tiedtke*, WM 1981, 1097; of other opinion *Zeranski*, JuS 2004, 340, 343.

case the transferee as a result of the real agreement[240] actually receives possession of the thing from a third party: again indirect possession will suffice.[241]
The requirement that the transferee actually obtains possession is indispensable, as otherwise the transfer of ownership could take place without the participation of a person who has been entrusted possession by the owner (or any of his intermediaries).[242] This of course would violate the *Veranlassungsprinzip*.

6. Requirements Regarding the Transferor

As mentioned above the fact that a person other than the owner is in possession of the thing must be the consequence of the owner's intention to entrust an intermediary or other third party. The fact that the legitimising appearance of the transferor's possession has occurred as a consequence of a deliberate action of the owner is one of the reasons which justify that the owner is burdened with the risk of loosing his property by a *bona fide*-acquisition and the corresponding preference for the reliability on legal transactions. This balance of interest relies on the possibility of the owner to decide to whom he wants to entrust his belongings and his better chance to judge the trustworthiness of his contracting partner or intermediary in comparison to purchaser, who has no information about the transferor.[243] A result of this principle is that *bona fide*-acquisition is excluded if the thing was either stolen or 'has become missing or otherwise lost'.
However, the requirement that the owner has deliberately entrusted another with the possession is already met, if the owner has handed over the thing to any other person. He need not himself have handed it over to the unauthorized transferor. Whether or not there is a further requirement that all further transfers of possession also have been deliberate is a matter of dispute (cf. *infra 8.*).
It should be mentioned that the requirement of deliberate transfer of possession does also apply both in case of sale in the ordinary course of business as well as to *bona fide*-acquisition under § 366 HGB.[244]
Two exceptions from this general rule are provided for: According to § 935 subsection 2 *bona fide*-acquisition concerning money and bearer securities is not ruled out by the fact that they have been stolen or otherwise have become missing. With respect to these instruments the interest of society in the ease and fluency of legal transactions prevails.[245]

---

240 *Baur/Stürner*, Sachenrecht[17], § 52 no. 22.
241 BGH DB 1969, 436; BGH NJW 1978, 696.
242 *Brehm/Berger*, Sachenrecht (2000), no. 27.63.
243 *Baur/Stürner*, Sachenrecht[17], § 52 no. 10.
244 *Handelsgesetzbuch* (Commercial Code).
245 *Quack* in: MünchKomm BGB[4], VI § 932 no. 5.

Money in the meaning of § 935 subsection 2 includes all valid means of payment. The term bearer instruments covers all negotiable instruments that grant the bearer the right to exercise the right recorded, such as bearer securities, debt certificates, theatre tickets, tickets for public transportation and stamps.

The second exception, also provided for in 935 subsection 2, covers the acquisition of goods stolen or otherwise missing in the course of a public auction. This provision is of particular importance in the context of stolen or confiscated works of art.[246] A public auction in the meaning of § 935 subsection 2 is a public auction defined in § 383 subsection 3 and therefore regularly a means of self-help sale.[247] The auction in the course of execution proceedings is not covered, as such an auction is provided for by the Civil Procedure Rules (§§ 814 ff. ZPO). The rules on *bona fide*-acquisition do not apply to such auction, as acquisition of ownership here is a consequence of the act of state, a special basis of original acquisition.[248]

7. Good faith

A further requirement of *bona fide*-acquisition from an unauthorized person under § 932 ff. is the good faith in respect of the ownership of the transferor. The good faith in regard of the authority to dispose will not suffice, unless the exception of the Commercial Code applies. According to § 366 HGB, a provision with a grand scope of practical relevance,[249] the good faith in the transferor's authority to dispose will also fulfil the requirement, if the transferor is a commercial agent and disposes of the goods in the regular course of his business.[250]

In case an agent acts in the place of the transferee the question whether or not the *bona fide*-requirement is fulfilled will depend on whether or not the agent is of good faith (cf. § 166 subsection 1).[251] This rule is modified in case the agent acts according to specific directions of the principal: in this case both, that is principal and agent, have to be in good faith (cf. § 166 subsection 2).[252] As far as the

---

246 Works of art which have been confiscated by the Nazi-Regime are held to ‚have become missing otherwise' in the meaning or § 935 subsection 1 and thus in general *bona fide*-acquisition is ruled out. However, in case of a public auction *bona fide*-acquisition is possible. For details see *Heuer*, NJW 1999, 2558, 2563 and *Müller-Katzenburg*, NJW 1999, 2551, 2555.

247 Cf. OLG München, NJW 1987, 1830.

248 RGZ 156, 395, 398.

249 *Quack* in: MünchKomm BGB^4 VI, § 932 no. 80.

250 The privilege of commerce as against to the general rules of private law therefore is only modest in comparison to other jurisdictions, cf. *Karner*, ZfRV 2004, 83, 85 (with further references).

251 *Quack* in: MünchKomm BGB^4 VI, § 932 no. 49.

252 *Baur/Stürner*, Sachenrecht^{17}, § 52 no. 32.

transferee is a juristic person the bad faith or negligence of one of the members of a body will be accounted to the juristic person.[253]

The required standard of good faith is defined by § 932 subsection 2: The acquirer is not in good faith, if he knows or owing to gross negligence does not know that the thing does not belong to the disposer. The existence of a relative prohibition to dispose dose not hinder a *bona fide*-acquisition, because the good faith of the transferee in the non-.existence of such prohibitions to dispose is also protected[254] (§ 135 subsection 2, § 136, § 2113 subsection 3). If the transferee, however, knows that the acquisition of the transferor is the result of a avoidable agreement, the bad faith with respect to this knowledge will preclude good faith in the meaning of § 932 subsection 2 (cf. § 142 subsection 2).[255]

Gross negligence according to the judicature of the Federal Supreme Court means that a transferor 'according to the circumstances has failed to observe the standard of care and has breached his duties in such a gross manner and has ignored what every person in the respective circumstances would have found quite obvious' (*die erforderliche Sorgfalt nach den gesamten Umständen in ungewöhnlich grobem Maße verletzt und dasjenige unbeachtet gelassen hat, was im gegebenen Fall jedem hätte einleuchten müssen*).[256] In case suspicious circumstances indicate that the transaction may not be authorized, a duty of information and examination will arise. The lack of observance of this duty will he held to involve gross negligence.

The scope of the duty of information and examination will *inter alia* depend on the circumstances and experience of the transferee. An experienced commercial businessman will have to live up to a more strict standard than a private person, who only rarely conducts similar transactions. The standard of care required will also depend on the type of transaction. Extraordinary contracts such as credit operations or a purchase in the open street will of course give rise to a more strict duty of examination than regular everyday purchases.[257] If as an example high priced goods are bought at a price considerably below the prime cost, then the purchaser may not simply rely on the information of the transferor that the goods have already been paid for. He has to undertake further inquiries in the authority of the seller.[258]

The judicature has developed detailed and strict rules for the purchase of cars, in particular second hand cars. A purchaser who buys a car without asking the transferor to hand over the registration certificate will as a general rule act grossly

[253] BGHZ 20, 149, 153; BGHZ 41, 282, 287.
[254] *Baur/Stürner*, Sachenrecht[17], § 52 no. 30.
[255] BGH NJW 1988, 482.
[256] BGHZ 10, 14, 16.
[257] *Quack* in: MünchKomm BGB[4] VI, § 932 no. 33 ff.
[258] BGH LM § 455 BGB Nr 23; cf. *Musielak*, JuS 1992, 713, 715.

negligent.[259] The same holds true for a person who buys a second-hand car and does not undertake any inquiries although the registration certificate received shows a third party as the registered user.[260]
The transferee must be in good faith at the time the transfer is completed,[261] *i.e.* the moment both real agreement and *traditio* are complete. In case the transfer is subject to a condition precedent, for instance the payment of the purchase price in case of a reservation-of-title-clause, the relevant point of time will still be real agreement and *traditio*, not the later moment the condition is met.[262]
The burden of proof lies on the party who denies the *bona fide*-acquisition, regularly the (former) owner. He will have to prove that the transferee was either *mala fide* or grossly negligent. If the factual situation cannot be reconstructed, the court in case of doubt will have to presume the good faith of the transferee.

8. Exclusion of Stolen Things and Such that Have Become Missing Otherwise

§ 935 subsection 1 excludes *bona fide*-acquisition of things that have been stolen from the owner or have become missing otherwise. The underlying idea of this exclusion is that in case a thing has been stolen or otherwise has become missing, the discrepancy between ownership and possession is not based on a deliberate act of the owner (*supra 1.*). The rule of § 935 also applies in the context of § 366 HGB.
A thing has become missing, if the owner has lost direct possession of it without a deliberate act.[263] The loss of possession therefore need not necessarily be contrary to his free will, but must have occurred without his (or his intermediary possessor's) consent.[264] Loss of possession without consent may also occur in case a person looses a thing or someone withholds possession from him. If the possessor is forced to give up possession by means of duress, this will also constitute loss of possession under § 935.
The consent to give up (direct) possession is not a legal act of the owner, but rather a natural act. Notwithstanding this categorization it is problematic to assess the intention of persons who either totally lack legal capacity or are of restricted legal capacity. Therefore a thing that has been given away by a person underage, who lacks legal capacity, is held to have become missing in the meaning of § 935

[259] BGHZ 10, 69, 74; BGHZ 30, 374, 380; BGH JZ 1965, 219; BGH NJW 1970, 653; BGH NJW 1981, 227 and OLG Düsseldorf NJW 1985, 2484, note by *Mittenzwei*, NJW 1986, 2472.
[260] BGH NJW 1994, 2022; quite similar BGH, NJW 1993, 1649 with note by *K Schmidt*, JuS 1993, 868.
[261] *Baur/Stürner*, Sachenrecht[17], § 52 no. 28.
[262] BGHZ 10, 69, 72 f.; BGHZ 30, 374, 377.
[263] *Baur/Stürner*, Sachenrecht[17], § 52 no. 37.
[264] *Quack* in: MünchKomm BGB[4] VI, § 935 no. 5; cf. *Baldus*, JR 2002, 441, 442 ff.

subsection 1. In case of a person with restricted capacity the assessment will depend on whether or not that person was able to understand the significance of the act.[265]

The requirement of involuntary loss of possession may be replaced by the involuntary loss of an intermediary possessor. If the direct possessor who holds possession in the name of the owner, however, gives up possession deliberately, although without the knowledge of the owner, the thing is not held to have become missing in the meaning of § 935 subsection 2.

In case a possessory servant deliberately transfers possession this will not constitute deliberate transfer by the possessor, because the possessory servant himself is not possessor.[266] Accordingly, the thing will be held to have become missing. The prevailing opinion confirms this rule and holds it to be applicable even in case the possessory servant had a position that – from a third party perspective – appeared as the position of an intermediary possessor. It is argued that the law does rely on the true factual possession and not on whether or not third parties could perceive that factual situation.[267]

Whether a thing has become missing, which the direct possessor involuntarily lost possession of, who does not hold possession with the intention to hold it for the owner is a matter of dispute.[268] According to a literal interpretation the possession of the owner was not involuntarily terminated as he has deliberately transferred possession to another. Therefore the prevailing opinion approves of the possibility of *bona fide*-acquisition.[269]

The consequence can be demonstrated by an example: Owner A gives his watch to B, who is supposed to repair it. However, B misappropriates the watch and hands it over to C, who cannot acquire ownership, because he is *mala fide*. Later on a thief D steals the watch from C and transfers it to E, who is in good faith. As the watch has not become missing from the owner A, because he has voluntarily transferred possession to B and E is *bona fide*, there is nothing to prevent a *bona fide*-acquisition under § 932 sentence 1.[270]

Things are also held to have become missing if the heirs are deemed to acquire possession under § 857 and a thing is taken from the estate. In case a presumptive

---

[265] *Baur/Stürner*, Sachenrecht[17], § 52 no. 42.

[266] *Witt*, AcP 201 (2001), 165, 180 ff.

[267] *Baur/Stürner*, Sachenrecht[17], § 52 no. 39; *Westermann/Gursky* § 49 I 6 (whereas in the previous edition it is argued in favour of the possibility of third parties to distinguish between possessory servant and direct possessor, *H. Westermann*, Sachenrecht[6] § 49 I 6); *Zeranski*, JuS 2004, 340, 344.

[268] Cf. *Braun*, JZ 1993, 391 ff.

[269] Palandt/*Bassenge* BGB[64], § 935 no. 2; *Quack* in: MünchKomm BGB[4] VI, § 935 no. 7; *Westermann/Gursky*, § 49 I 5; of other opinion *Baur/Stürner*, Sachenrecht[17], § 52 no. 38; *Braun*, JZ 1993, 391, 395 ff.; *Musielak*, JuS 1992, 713, 723.

[270] OLG Düsseldorf JZ 1951, 269.

heir sells a thing from the estate the purchaser can therefore not acquire ownership, unless the seller is authorized by a certificate of inheritance (cf. § 2366).
In case a thing has become missing, this permanently precludes *bona fide*-acquisition of ownership. Ownership and possession are permanently separated until either the original owner regains possession or the possessor acquires ownership by another mode of acquisition, for instance by specification or acquisitive prescription.[271] Of course, the exception concerning money or bearer instruments or acquisition by public auction according to § 935 subsection 2 is again applicable (cf. *supra 6)*.

9. Right to Re-Acquire Property

The result of *bona fide*-acquisition is that the transferee does acquire full and unburdened ownership. He therefore has all the rights provided for in § 903 and in particular can freely dispose of his property. A person who acquires property from a *bona fide*-acquirer therefore acquires from the authorized transferor, whether or not he knew that the transferor has acquired by *bona fide*-acquisition.[272] As the former owner has by the *bona fide*-acquisition lost all his rights in the property he cannot exercise any right to re-acquire his former property.[273]

10. *Bona Fide*-Acquisition Free of Encumbrances

§ 936 provides that, if a thing disposed of is encumbered with rights of third parties, these rights become extinguished upon acquisition of ownership, if the acquirer is *bona fide* with respect to such rights.
Encumbrances in the meaning of § 936 are all property rights other than ownership. As far as movable property is concerned therefore pledge and usufruct. Also equitable interest falls within this category.[274]
The requirements for *bona fide*-acquisition of ownership free of encumbrances are that one of the modes of acquisition of ownership according to § 929 ff. is met and that the transferee in addition acquires the form of possession required for the respective mode of *bona fide*-acquisition.[275] Whether the transferor is unauthorized or the authorized owner is without consequence.[276]

---

[271] *Baur/Stürner*, Sachenrecht[17], § 52 no. 46; *Quack* in: MünchKomm BGB[4] VI, § 935 no. 18.
[272] *Baur/Stürner*, Sachenrecht[17], § 52 no. 34.
[273] By contrast the draft version of § 939 provided that the *bona fide* acquirer could claim from the owner the amount he had paid to the unauthorized seller, cf. *Olzen*, Jura 1990, 505.
[274] *Zeranski*, AcP 203 (2003, 693, 698).
[275] *Baur/Stürner*, Sachenrecht[17], § 52 no. 52.
[276] *Baur/Stürner*, Sachenrecht[17], § 52 no. 52.

As in the context of § 932 ff., the transferee must be in good faith and the good faith must include the belief that the thing is unburdened by encumbrances. However, the conditions for *bona fide* in some cases are quite strict. The mere fact that a person obtained ownership in the premises of a lessee already was held to constitute bad faith.[277] § 367 HGB in addition precludes good faith of a banker.
A further requirement is that the thing has not become missing from the owner of the restricted property right, § 935 is applied *mutatis mutandis*:[278] if the owner takes a thing from his intermediary unauthorized and sells it to a third party, the thing has not become missing and *bona fide*-acquisition is as a rule not precluded. However, the thing has become missing from the possessor, therefore the requirement that the thing has been deliberately disposed of by the person whose right were extinguished by the *bona fide*-acquisition is not fulfilled. § 935 precludes the acquisition free of encumbrances under § 936: the purchaser acquires ownership, but ownership burdened by the rights of the former possessor who retains his property rights.
§ 936 subsection 3 also excludes the extinction of other property rights by *bona fide*-acquisition, if the transferee acquires ownership under the transfer mode of § 931, that is by means of assignment of the claim for recovery. The fact that the transferor is merely indirect possessor and a third party has direct possession already indicates that ownership is not unburdened, the acquisition of unburdened ownership therefore precluded (§ 936 subsection 3). The scope of this rule is extended to equitable interests, which will on fulfilment of a condition precedent or condition subsequent later be consolidated to full ownership.[279]
An further exception from the rules on acquisition of ownership free of encumbrances exists with respect to co-ownership: agreements on administration and use of common property will bind every subsequent acquirer of the share in co-ownership, whether or not he knew or should have known of their existence (§ 746).

§ 12. Prescription and Limitation of Action

1. Acquisition by Long Adverse Possession

The justification of the concept of acquisition by long adverse possession (acquisitive prescription) is to be found in the appreciation of the possessor's interest to be secure in his long lasting position, on the one hand, and the interest of society to hinder the permanent inconsistency between possession and

---

[277] BGH NJW 1972, 43; for criticism see *Baur/Stürner*, Sachenrecht[17], § 52 no. 52.
[278] *Baur/Stürner*, Sachenrecht[17], § 52 no. 52.
[279] For details see *Zeranski*, AcP 203 (2003), 693, 700 f.

ownership, on the other.[280] The German Civil Code does in contrast to Roman law not distinguish between regular and irregular prescription, but instead provides for a uniform concept of acquisitive prescription.[281]

The scope of application of course in practice is quite restricted, due to the acceptance of *bona fide*-acquisition from an unauthorized person.[282] The main relevance of acquisitive prescription today are cases where the possessor believes to have acquired derivative ownership, but in fact has not, because the good has either been stolen (or otherwise parted from the owner without his consent) in the meaning of § 935. Another reason may lie in a lack of legal capacity of the transferor/transferee.[283] Further, the lack of ownership of the recent possessor may stem from a defective original acquisition. The restricted importance of the concept of acquisitive prescription is reflected by the small number of reported cases on this subject.[284] From an economic perspective, acquisitive prescription is of some relevance in the context of works of art.[285]

Acquisitive prescription is provided for in § 937.

> **§ 937 BGB [Requirements of Acquisitive Prescription]**
>
> (1) A person, who has a movable thing in his proprietary possession for ten years acquires ownership (acquisitive prescription).
>
> (2) Acquisitive prescription is excluded, if the acquirer is not in good faith in obtaining possession or if he subsequently learns that he is not entitled to ownership.

Accordingly a person claiming original acquisition of ownership by acquisitive prescription has to comply with three requirements: (i) proprietary possession (*possessio*), (ii) good faith (*fides*) and (iii) lapse of time (*tempus*).

The first requirement of proprietary possession refers to § 872. Both direct and indirect possession will suffice.[286] As original acquisition does not constitute a legal act, legal capacity is not required.

The second requirement of good faith is fulfilled if the possessor *bona fide* believes that he is the owner of the goods in question, but does not require good faith in respect of the previous transferor.[287] Neither is a valid cause (*titulus iustus*) required. The possessor lacks *bona fide*, if he has either been grossly negligent or *mala fide* at the time of acquisition of possession or afterwards has

---

[280] *Baur/Stürner*, Sachenrecht[17], § 53 no. 85.

[281] Staudinger/*Wiegand* (2004), § 937 no. 1.

[282] *Baldus* in: MünchKomm BGB[4] VI, § 937 no. 1.; *Baur/Stürner*, Sachenrecht[17], § 53 no. 85.

[283] *Baldus* in: MünchKomm BGB[4], VI, § 937 no. 5.

[284] *Baur/Stürner*, Sachenrecht[17], § 53 no. 86.

[285] *Baldus* in: MünchKomm BGB[4] VI, § 937 no. 5; cf. *Finkenauer*, NJW 1998, 960 f.

[286] *Baldus* in: MünchKomm BGB[4] VI, § 937 no. 23.

[287] *Baldus* in: MünchKomm BGB[4] VI, § 937 no. 24.

gained actual knowledge that he has not acquired ownership. In case of looted art the acquirer will be held to be grossly negligent if he has not inquired about the origin of the respective works of art.[288]

Apart from possession and good faith the third requirement is that the time period has lapsed. According to § 937 the prescriptive period is 10 years and begins to run when the possessor *bona fide* acquires proprietary possession. A successor in title can rely on the period of proprietary possession of his legal predecessor (§ 943), if the successor does fulfil the other requirements, in particular *bona fide* proprietary possession.[289]

During the prescriptive period possession as a general rule has to be uninterrupted. Such uninterrupted possession of the proprietary possessor will be presumed according to § 938. In addition not every interruption of possession will actually interrupt the lapse of the time period: an interruption that occurs without the will of the possessor, and either is amended within a years time, or does lead to institution of an action for recovery within the same period will not be taken into account (§ 940). In case the prescriptive period is interrupted the effect is that the time expired before interruption is not calculated at all, but the period of 10 years will start afresh after the interruption has ended.

The prescriptive period is stayed, if revindication is claimed against the proprietary possessor (or his intermediary). The stay of the period for acquisitive prescription is computed according to the rules on the stay of prescription periods (§§ 203 ff.) and is effective only in relation to the person who claimed recovery. The prescriptive period is also stayed in case the prescription of the claim for revindication is stayed, either according to the general rules of prescription (§ 205-207), or at least the expiry of the prescription period is hindered according to §§ 210 ff. This in particular may occur in case the owner is by reason of law or of fact impeded to claim ownership.

If the possessor has complied with all three requirements, the legal consequence is that he acquires ownership free of any encumbrances (§ 937 in conjunction with § 945), if his good faith includes the believe that the property is unencumbered. In addition, it is also possible that the actual owner merely acquires freedom of encumbrance.

It is a matter of dispute, whether or not acquisitive prescription is a legal basis that protects the original acquisition of ownership against claims *ex* unjustified enrichment.[290] According to the prevailing opinion the answer depends on whether the claim is a *condictio sine causa* or a *condictio indebiti*: While a

---

[288] Cf. *Heuer*, NJW 1999, 2558, 2563 and *Müller-Katzenburg*, NJW 1999, 2551, 2556.

[289] Whether the *bona fide* heir of a *mala fide* testator can obtain ownership by acquisitive prescription, however, is a matter of dispute, see *Krämer*, NJW 1997, 2580 and the contrary opinion of *Finkenauer*, NJW 1998, 960.

[290] *Baldus* in: MünchKomm BGB[4] VI, § 937 no. 34.

condictio sine causa is held to be barred by acquisitive prescription a *condictio indebiti* is granted even after lapse of the prescription period.[291] The same applies to contractual claims. They will not be barred by acquisitive prescription.[292]
These problems have occurred due to the inconsistency of the long limitation period of thirty years, on the one hand, and the period for acquisitive prescription of ten years provided for in § 937, on the other. As the general long limitation period has been reduced to ten years by the law reform of 2002 (*Schuldrechtsmodernisierungsgesetz*) the problem has lost a lot of its former relevancy.[293]
As far as the burden of proof is concerned the possessor will have to assert and proof proprietary possession, as well as lapse of time (but in respect of the latter may rely on the presumption of uninterrupted possession and with regard to the former on § 1006), while the person claiming revindication will have to proof that the possessor lacks good faith.

2. Limitation of Ownership

Although the right of ownership itself is not terminated by limitation,[294] the claim to revindicate is subject to the general rules of limitation of action. According to § 197 subsection 1 no. 2 the limitation period for claims arising from ownership is 30 years. If this period has lapsed and the possessor invokes limitation, the owner does not actually loose his right to ownership, but can neither claim possession. In case the possessor cannot acquire ownership by acquisitive prescription – for example because he lacks good faith – right of ownership and right of possession will permanently fall apart.[295]

§ 13. Reservation of Title

1. The 'Simple' Reservation of Title

The concept of reservation of title consists of first, a contractual agreement containing a condition precedent that the transferor is not obliged to transfer ownership to the transferee before the later has paid the full purchase price and, second, a corresponding real agreement containing a reservation of title. However,

---

[291] Already held in RGZ 130, 69, 72 ff.; Staudinger/*Wiegand* (2004), § 937 no. 22; this is criticised by *Baldus* in: MünchKomm BGB[4] VI, § 937 no. 36.
[292] *Baldus* in: MünchKomm BGB[4] VI, § 937 no. 39.
[293] *Baldus* in: MünchKomm BGB[4] VI, § 937 no. 41; Staudinger/*Wiegand* (2004), § 937 no. 18.
[294] Hk-BGB/*Dörner*, § 195 no. 3.
[295] This is criticised by *Baldus* in: MünchKomm BGB[4] VI, § 937 no. 43.

as in property law in general, contractual agreement and real agreement have to be examined separately.

a) The Contractual Agreement (§ 449)

The concept of reservation of title has found express provision in § 449.

> **§ 449 BGB [Reservation of Title]**
>
> (1) If the seller has reserved title to a movable thing until payment of the purchase price, it is to be assumed, in case of doubt, that title will be transferred only upon payment of the purchase price in full, which constitutes a condition precedent (reservation of title).
>
> (2) Reservation of title entitles the seller to demand the surrender of thing only if he has terminated the contract.
>
> (3) An agreement on reservation of title is void inasmuch as the transfer of property is made conditional on the satisfaction by the buyer of third-party claims, in particular those of a business associated with the seller.

A contract of purchase containing a reservation of title is an unconditional agreement that obliges the transferor to transfer possession to the transferee and subsequently also transfer ownership as soon as the buyer has settled the full purchase price. A contractual agreement containing a reservation of title in general does neither require any specific formalities nor must the reservation be expressly agreed upon.[296] It can also form part of the general terms and conditions of trade, but will have to be in writing if the contracting party is a consumer (§ 502 subsection 1 no. 6).

It is a matter of long-lasting debate whether the fact that the seller performs his duty in advance and (at least) transfers possession to the buyer does on its own already imply a reservation of title, *i.e.* a conditional transfer of ownership. In legal doctrine it has been argued that the advance performance of the seller implies a reservation of title. This opinion mainly relies on § 320 subsection 1 which provides, that 'unless the contract requires him to perform first, a person bound by a synallagmatic contract may refuse to perform his part until the other party effects counter-performance [...]''. In case of deviation from the general rule of simultaneous performance, it is argued, a reservation of title is tacitly implied.[297]

Although judicature has long-since accepted the concept of a tacit reservation of title, it will not hold the mere advance performance sufficient to presume an

---

[296] HK-BGB/*Saenger*, § 449 no. 3.

[297] *Westermann* in: MünchKomm BGB[4] III, § 449 no. 15; Erman/*Grunewald*, § 449 no. 5.

implicit reservation, but will require further indications that point towards a tacit reservation of title.[298] As far as there are no such further indications the transfer of ownership in case of doubt will be held to be unconditional, even though the seller has performed in advance.[299]

If the contractual agreement does not contain a condition precedent, but the supplier of goods unilaterally declares a reservation of title after conclusion of contract (*e.g.* by means of sending his general terms and conditions of trade to the buyer) the condition is not validly agreed upon and will be held to be irrelevant.[300] The reservation of title does not form part of the contractual agreement.[301] Whether or not it is possible to agree upon a reservation of title *ex post facto* is again a matter of dispute.[302]

Such a reservation of title *ex post facto*, that is subsequent to an unconditional transfer, according to the judicature actually comprises first, an unconditional retransfer to the seller according to § 930 and second, a subsequent further – this time conditional – transfer to the buyer according to § 929 sentence 2.[303] Of course, regard has to be had to the requirement of a (re)transfer under § 930, namely the agreement of a valid relationship of constructive possession in the meaning of § 868. The mere agreement that the seller in future intends to possess the goods as a conditional purchaser will – according to judicature – not suffice.[304] Legal doctrine, by contrast, rejects this complicated construction and approves of an agreement of a reservation of title *ex post facto*,[305] though with the reservation that rights of third parties, which have arisen in the meantime, may not be affected.

b) The Conditional Real Agreement

On the level of property law a reservation of title is realized by a transfer of possession and a conditional real agreement containing the proviso that the transfer of ownership depends on the fulfilment of the condition precedent.[306] According to § 449 subsection 1 the fact that such a condition precedent has been

---

[298] BGH DB 1969, 1053; BGH DB 1977, 248.

[299] Erman/*Grunewald*, § 449 no. 5; of other opinion *Westermann* in: MünchKomm BGB[4] III, § 449 no. 15.

[300] For the possible effects on the real agreement cf. *infra 2*.

[301] *Baur/Stürner*, Sachenrecht[17], § 59 no. 11.

[302] Contrary BGH NJW 1953, 217; but agreed to by *Baur/Stürner*, Sachenrecht[17], § 59 no. 11.

[303] BGH NJW 1953, 217; *Baur/Stürner*, Sachenrecht[17], § 51 no. 34; *Westermann* in: MünchKomm BGB[4] III, § 449 no. 19 ff.

[304] RGZ 54, 396; RGZ 49, 170; BGH NJW 1953, 217; this point deliberately was left undecided in BGHZ 42, 53, 58; for criticism see *Westermann* in: MünchKomm BGB[4] III, § 449 no. 19.

[305] *Baur/Stürner*, Sachenrecht[17], § 51 no. 34.

[306] *Westermann* in: MünchKomm BGB[4] III, § 449 no. 13.

validly agreed upon (and therefore forms an integral part of the contractual agreement) leads to a legal presumption that the real agreement also contains a respective condition precedent.

This will even apply in case the transfer of possession does not take place simultaneously with the conclusion of the contract, but some time later: the reservation of title contained in the contractual agreement is implicitly extended to the real agreement without requiring further express agreement.[307]

As mentioned above, the fact that the seller after conclusion of the contract sends the purchaser his general terms and conditions of sale implying a reservation of title (or provides such at delivery with similar content) will not alter the contractual agreement. However, the reservation of title may become part of the real agreement, if the seller points to the conditional transfer and the purchaser does not object.[308]

A seller who asserts that a reservation of title has been agreed upon, although the purchaser claims that the transfer has been performed without reservation, will be burdened with the onus of proof by reason of the legal presumption of § 1006.[309]

c) The Legal Consequences

Until the condition of full payment of purchase price is met, the seller will remain owner of the goods, but by reason of the conditional transfer is restricted in his power to dispose (§ 161).[310]

Notwithstanding the ownership of the seller the conditional purchaser has already acquired a secure legal position: § 160 subsection 1 and § 161 subsection1 1st sentence protect him against disposition or other detrimental acts of the conditional seller. In addition the conditional purchaser is the lawful possessor of the goods and therefore can invoke all the protective measures provided for in § 858 ff. A claim for surrender by the conditional seller or a third party can be rejected by recourse to his right to possession (§ 986 subsection 2). Granted an equitable interest he is similarly protected against third party interference by (analogous) application of §§ 823, 985 and § 1004.

As long as the purchaser fulfils all his contractual duties, in particular regularly pays the instalments of the purchase price, the seller – although the legal owner – only has a right to ask payment, but may not claim recovery of the goods.[311] Even in case of non-payment, default of payment or insolvency this malperformance on

---

307 *Baur/Stürner*, Sachenrecht[17], § 59 no. 12.

308 BGH NJW 1979, 213; BGH NJW 1979, 2199; BGH NJW 1982, 1749. *Westermann* in: MünchKomm BGB[4] III, § 449 no. 18.

309 BGH NJW 1975, 1269; BGHZ 64, 395, 396 f.

310 *Westermann* in: MünchKomm BGB[4] III, § 449 no. 7.

311 *Westermann* in: MünchKomm BGB[4] III, § 449 no. 33.

its own does not constitute a right of the seller to revindicate. According to § 449 subsection 2 a further requirement is that the seller has validly terminated the contract. The underlying objective of this rule is to protect the purchaser from the situation, that the seller simultaneously claims surrender of the goods as well as payment and thereby deprives the purchaser of his right to use the goods, which will often reduce his chance to acquire the monies he needs to satisfy the seller.[312] But of course the purchaser's default grants the seller a right to terminate the contract according to the general rules (cf. § 323).
The purchaser will often be interested to dispose of the value acquired by his instalments. The legal order does acknowledge this interest and accordingly grants the conditional purchaser a conditional future interest, *i.e.* an equitable interest (*Anwartschaftsrecht*).[313] According to the prevailing doctrine it is a right *in rem*[314] and can independently be transferred to third parties. Consequently the rules of transfer of this '*Anwartschaftsrecht*' do not follow the rules on assignment, but rather the rules on transfer of ownership (cf. *supra § 1 4.*).[315]
Yet, an important distinction between the equitable interest and ownership has to be kept in mind: the existence of the equitable interest depends on the possibility that the condition precedent may still be complied with. If for instance the seller terminates the contract for default of payment, the contract is void and the condition can no longer be satisfied. The equitable interest ceases to exist, whether or not it has been transferred to a third party.[316]

d) The Relinquishment of Reservation of Title

The reservation of title is relinquished *ex nunc* if the condition precedent is fulfilled.[317] Simultaneously the equitable interest is converted into full ownership. If the equitable interest has been transferred to a third party, the conditional purchaser does not first acquire ownership for a logical second, but the third party directly acquires ownership (*Direkterwerb*).[318]
Other reasons of relinquishment of the reservation of title may be that the conditional purchaser resells the goods to third parties with prior approval of the conditional seller (§ 185): in this case the third party acquires full ownership

---

312 BGHZ 54, 214, 220 f.; BGH JZ 1989, 199; *Westermann* in: MünchKomm BGB[4] III, § 449 no. 33. See also *Habersack/Schürnbrand*, JuS 2002, 833, 836.
313 *Baur/Stürner*, Sachenrecht[17], § 59 no. 3.
314 *Baur/Stürner*, Sachenrecht[17], § 59 no. 4; *Westermann* in: MünchKomm BGB[4] III, § 449 no. 42 (with further references).
315 *Baur/Stürner*, Sachenrecht[17], § 59 no. 34.
316 BGHZ 75, 221, 225 f.; *Baur/Stürner*, Sachenrecht[17], § 59 no. 19.
317 *Westermann* in: MünchKomm BGB[4] III, § 449 no. 23.
318 BGHZ 20, 88; BGHZ 28, 16, 22; *Westermann* in: MünchKomm BGB[4] III, § 449 no. 53.

without reservation. Such prior approval is presumed, if the conditional seller is a resale business.[319]
The reserved ownership of the seller will further cease in case of original acquisition by a third party, for instance in case of specification (§ 950) or good faith acquisition (§ 932 ff.).[320] By contrast limitation of action in respect of the claim for the purchase price will not affect the seller's right of ownership.

e) Execution and Insolvency

In case the conditional purchaser is unable to settle his debts and the conditional seller is afraid that other creditors may try to realize the value of the goods purchased under reservation of title, the remedies differ between enforcement proceedings and insolvency.
Levy of execution by other creditors with respect to the goods purchased under reservation of title can be resisted by means of a third-party intervention against execution (§ 771 ZPO).[321] The purchaser's creditors therefore can only realize the value of the goods if they settle the remaining instalments.
In case of insolvency of the conditional purchaser the insolvency administrator according to § 103 subsection 1 InsO may choose, whether he settles the remaining purchase price or refuses fulfilment of the contract and grants release of the goods from estate (§ 47 InsO). If the conditional seller claims release from estate, he has to return the instalments already paid to the bankruptcy's estate, but may deduct from that sum a compensation for use. In case the insolvent party is the conditional seller, the insolvency administrator's choice is reduced (§ 107 subsection 1): the purchaser may still acquire ownership, if he settles the instalments left.

2. The Void/Avoidable Reservation of Title

In order to be fully effective a reservation of title will have to be part of both the contractual and the real agreement. The consequences of a lack of a respective reservation in one of the agreements depends on which agreement is concerned by this defect.
In case the sales contract does not contain a (valid) reservation of title, the consequence will be that the seller is under a contractual duty to transfer unreserved ownership. If he – contrary to this duty – only transfers possession and

---

[319] BGH NJW 1991, 228.
[320] In order to prevent this result, the owner who transfers a car under reservation of title in practice retains the registration card and thereby prevents the good faith of a subsequent purchaser, cf. *Westermann* in: MünchKomm BGB[4] III, § 449 no. 10 and § 11 7.
[321] *Westermann* in: MünchKomm BGB[4] III, § 449 no. 75.

reserves the title of ownership in the real agreement, he has not fulfilled the standard obligations of the seller (§ 433): the purchaser may claim unreserved transfer of ownership.

Whether the purchaser in this case does not acquire ownership at all or does at least acquire an equitable interest, will depend on whether or not he does agree with the seller's declaration of reservation of ownership (at least insofar as necessary to constitute a valid real agreement).[322] If he does not consent to the reservation there is no valid real agreement. The purchaser neither acquires ownership nor an *Anwartschaftsrecht.*[323]

In case the seller according to the underlying contractual agreement was only under a duty to transfer conditional ownership, but actually has transferred unreserved ownership, the purchaser acquires the right of ownership. The seller though may claim retransfer *ex* unjustified enrichment, because the transfer is *sine causa* (§ 812 subsection 1 Sentence 1). However, this case will rarely occur, because due to the rule provided in § 449 subsection 1 a reserved transfer will be presumed in case the contractual agreement contains a respective reservation of title.

3. Extended Reservation of Title

As mentioned above a mere reservation of title as a rule only prevents a derivative transfer of ownership prior to full payment of the purchase price, but cannot hinder original acquisition by *commixtio* or *specificatio*. Legal practice therefore has developed the concept of an extended reservation of title. It is of particular importance in the context of supplier's credit.[324] Such an extended reservation of ownership is not expressly provided for by law and according to the judicature requires an express agreement to that end.[325]

An extended reservation of title is composed of a valid agreement of a reservation of title as set out above and an additional prior approval of the seller, which permits the purchaser to resell the goods in the usual course of business. The purchaser in turn in advance assigns the claims for the purchase price he receives in return to the seller as substitute security (*Vorausabtretungsklausel*).

As far as the purchaser is not a resale business, but rather a manufacturer and accordingly does not resell the goods but produces new goods, a similar result may be achieved by agreement on a processing clause (*Verarbeitungsklausel*) in

---

322 HK-BGB/*Saenger*, § 449 no. 3.

323 BGH NJW 1953, 217; BGHZ 64, 395, 397.

324 *Westermann* in: MünchKomm BGB[4] III, § 449 no. 1.

325 Cf. Palandt/*Putzo*[64] § 449 no. 19; of other opinion *Nierwetberg*, NJW 1983, 2235, 2236, who argues in favour of acceptance of tacit agreements if such is covered by the intention of the parties.

addition to an anticipated further conditional transfer of ownership to the manufacturer.[326] By means of the processing clause the supplier is held to be the producer in the meaning of § 950 and accordingly acquires original ownership of the products manufactured. In order to create the same property rights in the products as have existed prior to specification, the supplier now transfers conditional ownership of the products to the manufacturer.
Judged from an economic perspective, it is quite obvious that the extended reservation of ownership is not actually a reservation of ownership, as the main interest of the seller is not to revindicate but to acquire security for the unsettled instalments of the purchase price. This aspect is taken into account in case of insolvency. The extended reservation of ownership will be treated similarly to a fiduciary transfer of ownership: the seller will not be granted a right to claim release from estate but only a claim for segregation from estate (cf. *supra § 8 2. c*).[327]

4. Expanded Reservation of Title

An expanded reservation of title means that the seller reserves the title of ownership, but alters the condition precedent. The purchaser will not acquire ownership, unless he settles not only the purchase price but also other debts. Such other debts covered by the agreement may for instance be future debts arising from the same business relationship. The expanded reservation of title is in general held to be valid, however, judicature construes it narrowly.[328] By contrast an agreement on reservation of title made conditional on the satisfaction of third-party claims, in particular those of a business associated with the seller, is void according to the express provision of § 449 subsection 3.[329]

---

[326] Cf. *Nierwetberg*, NJW 1983, 2235.
[327] BGH JZ 1971, 505 (extended reservation of title); BGH JZ 1971, 506 (expanded reservation of title).
[328] Cf. *Westermann* in: MünchKomm BGB[4] III, § 449 no. 82 ff.
[329] Cf. *Habersack/Schürnbrand*, JuS 2002, 833, 837 f.

Salzburger Studien zum Europäischen Privatrecht

Herausgegeben von J. Michael Rainer

Band 1 Marc Herzog: Die Haftung des Gastwirts für eingebrachte Sachen des Gasts nach §§ 701 - 703 des Deutschen Bürgerlichen Gesetzbuchs. 1999.

Band 2 Andreas Reinhart: Familienplanungsschaden. Wrongful birth, wrongful life, wrongful conception, wrongful pregnancy. Eine rechtsvergleichende Untersuchung anhand des deutschen und des anglo-amerikanischen Rechts. 1999.

Band 3 Markus Frank: Untersuchungen zu den *Politika* des Aristoteles. 1999.

Band 4 Stefan Josef Schermaier: Der Gemeinschaftsrechtliche Staatshaftungsanspruch. Entwicklung, Perspektiven und Auswirkungen auf das österreichische Recht. 1999.

Band 5 Carmen Windhaber: Reiserecht in Österreich, Deutschland und Kanada. 2000.

Band 6 Korbinian Dietl: Unfallhaftung beim Expeditions- und Trekkingbergsteigen. Zugleich ein Beitrag zum Reiserecht für den Bereich der Bergreisen sowie zum Sporthaftungsrecht für den Bereich des Bergsports. 2000.

Band 7 Erich Jeroscheg: Eigentum an beweglichen Sachen. Französisches Recht und Rechtsvergleich. 2000.

Band 8 Thomas Tschaler: Das Moment der Gefahr als Element der Schadenszurechnung im System des Haftpflichtrechts. Eine rechtstheoretische Untersuchung der möglichen Schwächen gängiger Haftungsmodelle. 2000.

Band 9 Christian Hellenthal: Zulässigkeit einer supranationalen Fußball-Europaliga nach den Bestimmungen des europäischen Wettbewerbsrechts. 2000.

Band 10 Wolfgang Bengen: Die Systematik des § 823 I BGB im Deliktsrecht. Zugleich ein Beitrag zu den Verkehrspflichten. 2000.

Band 11 Gerhard Pöttler: Vergleichende Verbraucherschutzrichtlinienumsetzung in europäischen Mitgliedsstaaten. Anhand ausgewählter Beispiele der Pauschalreise-, Timesharing- und Produkthaftungsrichtlinie. 2001.

Band 12 Johannes Michael Rainer: Europäisches Privatrecht. Die Rechtsvergleichung. 2002.

Band 13 Erwin Schön: Allgemeines Vertragsrecht und Kaufvertragsrecht - ein Rechtsvergleich Österreich, USA, Spanien und UN-Kaufrecht. Unter Einbeziehung von PECL und UNIDROIT-Prinzipien. Gemeinsamkeiten, Unterschiede, Bewertungsversuche. 2003.

Band 14 Patrick Schenner: Skiunfall! Wer haftet? Schadenersatz im österreichischen Skirecht. 2003.

Band 15 Peter Unterkofler: Die rechtliche Stellung des Pflichtteilsberechtigten im Spannungsverhältnis zwischen Erbrecht und Privatstiftungsrecht. 2003.

Band 16 Susanne Spaun: Der Herausgabeanspruch bei Diebstahl oder illegalem Export von Kulturgütern. 2003.

Band 17 Josef Wolff: Trust, Fiducia und fiduziarische Treuhand. Historisch-rechtsvergleichende Untersuchung mit einer Darstellung des Trust in Schottland sowie des römischen und österreichischen Fideikommiss. 2005.

Band 18 Johannes Michael Rainer / Johanna Filip-Fröschl: Transfer of Title Concerning Movables Part I – Eigentumsübertragung an beweglichen Sachen in Europa Teil I. Introduction, Estonia, Italy, Poland, Portugal, Scotland, Slovenia. Einführung, Estland, Italien, Polen, Portugal, Schottland, Slowenien. Edited by Johannes Michael Rainer – Herausgegeben von Johannes Michael Rainer. 2006.

Band 19 Mary-Rose McGuire: Transfer of Title Concerning Movables Part II – Eigentumsübertragung an beweglichen Sachen in Europa Teil II. National Report: Germany. Edited by Johannes Michael Rainer – Herausgegeben von Johannes Michael Rainer. 2006.

Band 20 Claes Martinson: Transfer of Title Concerning Movables Part III – Eigentumsübertragung an beweglichen Sachen in Europa Teil III. National Report: Sweden. Edited by Johannes Michael Rainer – Herausgegeben von Johannes Michael Rainer. 2006.

Band 21 Arthur Salomons: Transfer of Title Concerning Movables Part IV – Eigentumsübertragung an beweglichen Sachen in Europa Teil IV. National Report: The Netherlands. Edited by Johannes Michael Rainer – Herausgegeben von Johannes Michael Rainer. 2006.

www.peterlang.de

Stefan Sauer

Eigentumsschutz und Verfassungsstruktur in Indien

Frankfurt am Main, Berlin, Bern, Bruxelles, New York, Oxford, Wien, 2004.
XXI, 275 S.
Europäische Hochschulschriften: Reihe 2, Rechtswissenschaft. Bd. 3961
ISBN 3-631-52164-2 · br. € 51.50*

In Indien war das Recht auf Eigentum aufgrund seiner Bedeutung für die zukünftige Wirtschaftsordnung des Landes eines der umstrittensten Grundrechte überhaupt, das 1950 Eingang in die neue Verfassung gefunden hat. 1978 wurden die Eigentumsartikel aus dem Grundrechtsteil gestrichen und in modifizierter Form an anderer Stelle in der Verfassung geregelt. Entgegen gandhianischer Eigentumsphilosophie wird das Recht auf Eigentum heute grundsätzlich als Menschenrecht anerkannt. Die Debatte um die Eigentumsartikel führte zur Klärung grundlegender Strukturen des indischen Verfassungsstaates. Neben der Reichweite des Eigentumsschutzes sind sein Verhältnis zu gegenläufigen Staatszielbestimmungen und die Grenzen der Verfassungsänderung weitere Themen der vergleichenden Betrachtung.

Aus dem Inhalt: *Permanent Settlement* (1793) · *Government of India Act* (1935) · Verfassung von 1950 · Entwicklung der Eigentumsartikel bis 1978 · Eigentum und Eigentumsschutz nach 1978 · Grundrechtsbeschwerde und *Writ*-Verfahren · Eigentumsschutz und Verfassungsstruktur · Allgemeine Eigentumsdogmatik · Eigentum und Staatszielbestimmungen · Eigentum und Verfassungsänderung

Kolibri 360 GmbH
Ferdinand-Jühlke-Straße 7
99095 Erfurt, Deutschland
produktsicherheit@kolibri360.de

Druck:
CPI Druckdienstleistungen GmbH
im Auftrag der
Kolibri 360 GmbH
Ferdinand-Jühlke-Str. 7
99095 Erfurt